Wanna Teach PE?

The A-Z Guide for People that
'Wanna Teach PE'

Written for the next generation
of aspiring teachers.

By Ben Holden

First published in 2022 by Scholary
The Dutch Barn, Bremhill Grove Farm, Chippenham, Wiltshire, SN15 4LX, United Kingdom

Scholary is an imprint of Scholary Ltd

Typeset in Avenir

British Library Cataloguing in Publication Data.
A catalogue record for this book is available from the British Library.

ISBN: 978-1-9999-0925-3 (pbk)
ISBN: 978-1-9999-0926-0 (hbk)
ISBN: 978-1-9999-0927-7 (ebk)

Table of Contents

Dedication

From sitting down, opening the laptop, and writing those first few words, to being in a position of having a book that will be able to help so many people working in the profession has been a long journey but, thankfully, it has not been a journey I have taken alone.

There are a number of people that I would like to personally thank for their support and insight in writing this book.

A huge thank you to Dr Liz Durden-Myers and Will Swaithes for firstly taking a punt on me, and for their unwavering guidance throughout each stage of the book's creation. A big thank you to Tracey Healey for her expertise and guidance in her review of the book also.

Thank you to Sue Wilkinson MBE for providing such a passionate and inspiring foreword for the book, along with the army of people from the world of PE that have provided such fantastic reflections on each chapter.

A special mention to my mentors that guided me during the infancy of my PE teaching career. Warren, Jon, Julie, Danny, Mike, Peter, Mark and Dave, thank you.

A huge thank you to all my colleagues whom I have worked alongside and learned so much from during my time at High Tunstall – so proud of our continuing journey! Not to forget the brilliant pupils that have provided so much joy to teaching.

And, finally, the most sincere acknowledgements to my family. My beautiful children, Penny and Ossie, my late Dad Jack for his unwavering support of my sporting and life endeavours, and to the three main ladies in my life, Linda, Mum and, my greatest supporter, my wife Fiona.

Foreword

Sue Wilkinson MBE
CEO of the Association for Physical Education (AfPE)

At a time when the world has faced a pandemic, like nothing we have ever seen before, plus horrendous challenges across other parts of the world, the physical and emotional well-being of young people has to be front and centre in their education. A great many educationalists recognise that physical education (PE), whilst it cannot be the 'Swiss army knife' to mend societal ills, can make a significant contribution to the physical, social, emotional, and cognitive development of all those in an educational setting.

The importance of the subject has been exemplified during the events of the past two years; it is a statutory entitlement from 5 to 16 in England. The government too has recognised the importance of the subject, with Will Quince, the Parliamentary under Secretary of State (Minister for Children and Families), during a response to the Westminster 'PE as a core subject' debate, led by Edward Timpson, CBE MP, stating that 'healthy' literacy is extremely important. PE has a significant role to play as part of the solution in the holistic approach to the challenges faced. The AfPE Task Force, chaired by Edward, brought colleagues together from across the sector, but also from the medical world, to investigate the importance and contribution of PE, whilst collecting evidence from the workforce who lead and teach the subject. As a result, it was felt unanimously that, as we know, the subject is of exponential importance to every child and young person's development. One of the main recommendations is that PE should be a core subject or, at the very least, have the status of literacy and numeracy, and be placed at the heart of school life.

In AfPE, we believe in being positive, and that there is no point in looking back and complaining. We must look forward, celebrate and advocate what is making a difference in schools and ensure PE does not succumb to any further reductions in time on the curriculum – that its status is elevated, and all teachers of PE are valued and respected. This will require all within the sector and beyond to work in collaboration, ensuring that governors, senior leadership teams, parents, pupils and the teaching workforce, all own the curriculum, that they can articulate it, and know and understand the impact it can have on young people's lives. We must ensure, whilst being realistic, that we design a strategy to ensure PE is well-planned, ambitious, understood and resourced. This vision or intent must be visible, because otherwise it cannot be seen. However, we have all seen a plethora of great strategies, but a strategy without effective execution (implementation) is nothing short of a hallucination, and then the impact cannot be realised. The quality of teaching and learning in schools lies at the very heart of success; this is crucial to ensure pupils are inspired to enjoy learning in and through physical education.

Michael J Fox said, ' I am careful not to confuse excellence with perfection…' This is key, as every PE, sport, and physical activity (PESSPA) professional strives for excellence, but we cannot always be perfect, and we must not be afraid to trial new ideas and make mistakes, but instead learn from our experiences. However, by continually trying, testing, and learning we will be able to improve the quality of young people's lives – we cannot stand back and do nothing. It is never easy, but PESSPA professionals must continually demonstrate their innovative and creative ideas, whilst remaining resilient and committed to those in their charge. Senior leaders and governors must understand that investment in PESSPA professionals is a priority if we are to ensure pupils remain safe, secure, physically and emotionally well, and motivated to strive for excellence.

Valuing and nurturing well-being has been a priority for everyone; however, well-being is an outcome of excellent physical education and physical activity, being offered in an inclusive way. It will secure a significantly greater outcome when the subject is embedded across the whole school, and is part of school culture with 100% buy-in from the whole community. We must be consistent in our definitions and focus clearly on outcomes for young people, so that they leave school being the best individuals they can.

I am in no doubt that the role of the subject leader and the school workforce are vital if PE is to be the transformative subject that we all know it is. We are realists, and recognise that the workforce is under a phenomenal amount of pressure, but this must be streamlined, resourced, and managed. PE is the key to unlocking the secret garden of better physical and emotional well-being whilst achieving outcomes such as improved confidence, better decision making and leadership skills, the ability to work as a team, and being able to work independently, to name but a few examples.

So, to conclude, the question isn't, 'who is going to let us place PE at the front and centre of the curriculum', it's, 'who is going to stop us?' Because, if we do not move in collaboration to achieve this, I dread to think of the impact on future generations, both physically and emotionally, in addition to those other vital life skills that PE makes such a significant contribution to whilst young people are in the education system.

This book contains a plethora of information, which forms the ingredients for you to design a bespoke menu for the provision of an ambitious, sequenced, and progressive PE curriculum for all.

Sue Wilkinson MBE, FRSA

Preface

As soon as the plane touched down at Heathrow, I remember feeling an incredible level of anxiety. I was back in my home country, with the same bag on my shoulder that I had left with 12 months earlier. But this time, as I stepped off the plane, I had no plan, no employment, no excitement, and no idea what my next steps would be.

It was the first time that my life was not moving in a linear direction towards a target. Be it working towards my GCSEs, A Levels, or through each year of University, I'd always been moving closer to a personal or academic goal. This time, however, I sat in the Airport arrivals lounge, waiting for my lift back up North, overwhelmed by that daunting thought of 'what next?'.

To provide some context, without this turning into a glorified 'This is your Life', I'd coached 'soccer' in the USA during each of my university summer holiday periods. Upon completion of my degree, the company I worked with offered me a full-time position coaching and co-ordinating 'soccer' delivery in Los Angeles.

The experience was incredible, to be able to live in a different culture as a 21-year-old was not only a real coming of age, sink or swim challenge, but it also provided me with a foundation and insight into physical activity delivery. I was able to observe some fantastically talented coaches, and many of the techniques I learned still underpin my practice to this day.

There was a feeling throughout my time in America that, although the experiences and memories being made would be lifelong, deep down I knew my future would follow a different path to the avenues on offer in the United States. Therefore, I believe fate intervened in several ways. The company I worked for became insolvent, and my father fell seriously ill, meaning that my time abroad would be cut short and I was going to need a 'Life Plan B'. I had several years' coaching experience; PE teaching would be a good idea, surely?

As a sports-obsessed child, throughout school, PE was the lesson I hunted out on the day timetables were handed out. Immediately, whatever day of the week that you had PE was always going to be the best day of the week. Then there was this person that got to play sports all day, an almost God-like figure, and they got to pick the sports teams too – they were just the coolest person ever!

I mean, do not get me wrong, us PE teachers are a cool breed! We also get to do those cool things that the adolescent me thought was the entirety of teaching. Teaching here is so much more beneath the surface than a Key Stage 3 PE class will ever appreciate. This book is intended to provide ideas and strategies, whilst assisting you in conceptualising what being a PE teacher is all about.

Being a PE teacher is the greatest job in the world. I am incredibly lucky to work in an amazing school in the North-East of England, with fantastic pupils from a diverse demographic. I have also had the opportunity to work alongside many talented colleagues, each with their own skill sets, strategies, and ideas that help them to be outstanding practitioners of physical education.

Having worked in physical education for the past 12 years, I have worn many different hats. From gifted and talented coordinator, to leading ICT across the curriculum, working as a Specialist Leader for Education (SLE) for physical education across our region since 2013, and I have been lucky to work in my dream job, as a Head of physical education. I feel extremely grateful to be able to lead a team of talented practitioners that share my vision for the subject.

Additionally, I have also been a mentor for many trainee teachers, wishing to embark on a career in PE teaching. Each chapter within this book is denominated a letter of the alphabet, and inspired by aspects of previous trainees' practice that required further development or an alternative approach.

Sometimes, trainees are appreciative of feedback provided, reflect, and make the necessary steps to work on the highlighted aspect of their teaching and further refine their craft. Sadly, sometimes, trainees can be averse to feedback, see it as an attack, and fail to demonstrate the resilience required to act upon it. Reflective practice is paramount. Reflective trainees with a willingness to embrace feedback and trial new actions in future lessons are always the most successful. The most positive and successful mentor-mentee relationships shape the messages and advice that are shared within each chapter, from a range of mentors and their experiences.

The chapters take inspiration from the shop floor: sports halls, gyms, courts and sports fields, that host thousands of lessons every year. They are inspired by the experiences of learners, their feedback, and the occasional anecdotal recollection that will help you to appreciate some of that deeper thinking and consideration that goes on behind the scenes of great PE lessons.

This book will not automatically make you 'The Ultimate PE Teacher'. Teaching perfection does not exist. I have never taught the perfect lesson but if by the end of this book you have a moment of teaching inspiration, when you are 25 minutes into lesson 3, half way through November, in the 4th year of your teaching career, that helps to improve the physical education experience of the young people in your lesson, then taking the time to write this book will have been worthwhile.

A

Active

Activity levels within lessons are crucial, but activity for activity's sake is not. Remember, we are educating the physical, not merely facilitating low stakes movement. Inclusive, high quality activity time in lessons should be at the forefront of thought and planning ahead of all physical education Lessons.

When entrusted with the role of being a PE teacher, it is worth taking a moment to reflect upon your own teaching philosophy, by asking yourself: what is the aim of physical education, and how will I achieve this aim? Hopefully being active now and later in life have featured in your thoughts. You are given a set amount of time within a day and within a week to create an environment to achieve this aim. As such, it is imperative that you maximise the amount of high-quality activity time within your lessons.

Some time ago, Sky Sports offered a 'Player Cam' option to their viewers. The basic premise was that people could select an option with a camera homed in on an individual player for the entirety of the match. This concept is a useful idea when it comes to teaching PE. If you were to 'Player Cam' a student within your lesson, for how much of the lesson time would they be active? For how much of the lesson are they static? Awaiting a turn, listening to an instruction, answering a register? Lessons naturally have elements where it is more difficult for them to be active; it is therefore crucial that lesson design focuses on getting young people moving and learning.

If we consider that a PE lesson is on average 1 hour in length; once, realistically, 20 minutes are deducted for changing time and registers being taken (along with the inevitable 3 notes from home and the 2 pupils that have forgotten their trainers), you are left with 40 minutes to work with. Then, in this 40-minute timeframe, you're going to need to introduce the lesson concept, the bigger picture, the objectives, leave time for questioning, whilst also incorporating a plenary towards the end. It's probably at this stage when we write everything down, that you are beginning to realise that more and more activity time is being eaten into and, as such, some 'PE Lessons' are becoming not that physical at all.

Taking everything into consideration, some guidance that I have provided for our teachers is to aim for 30 minutes of 'moderate intensity' activity time in each lesson. Now, this is not a concrete prerequisite, as there will be plenty of situations within lessons that will eat into this further. A pupil failing to grasp a concept, low level disruption, an injury, but if in every lesson PE teachers are consciously considering the amount of activity time that will exist in a lesson at the planning stage, this can only lead to lessons helping young people work towards achieving the government recommendation of 1 hour's moderate exercise every day. Within primary PE, this focus on maximising activity time is vital, especially given the length of changing time commonly associated with younger pupils. Playing a song during changing time and challenging all pupils to be ready before it finishes can be a subtle yet effective method of speeding up changing time in both primary and secondary PE lessons. Once consideration has been given to how to achieve more/higher activity levels, the next challenge is to ensure that the activity is relevant, purposeful, and working towards the overall aim of the curriculum and/or individual lesson.

There are many subtle ways to maximise activity time within lessons. Later in the book, I mention my hate of 'queueing' in PE lessons – this is simply an avoidable period of inactivity. Instead of young people waiting a turn, consider how queues can be removed, or how pupils can be active whilst awaiting their turn, if it is an activity that is a traditional 'turn taker', such as trampolining or long jump. If we take the trampolining example, in a class of 25 pupils and 3 trampoline beds, it would be perfectly safe for 4 pupils per bed to act as spotters along with 3 young people performing. This leaves 10 pupils. Instead of having these pupils as spotters, could they be working through an alternative activity? Muscular conditioning, partner balances or shape development on the floor. Whilst appreciating there might be space issues, I am simply trying to illustrate the concept of considering how activity time could be maximised.

Take the long jump. You can all picture the standard long jump lesson. Teacher stood next to the pit, beckoning student after student into the pit before telling them a very quick and rough estimate of their distance. Pupils patiently waiting their turn, or not so patiently, as low-level disruption begins. Pupils become cold and, as they are 20 metres down the runway, the opportunity for any form of peer assessment is lost too. Consider what activities pupils could be undertaking whilst they await their turn, could you set up several stations on the return to the queue? A speed, agility and quickness station, standing long jump challenge, or a station where pupils check their approach length? Now the time spent inactive is drastically reduced, a teacher can still focus on providing that crucial personalised feedback, and be content in the knowledge that, following a warm-up and skill development, the magic 30 minutes activity time is even being hit in a traditionally inactive lesson like the long jump.

In addition to lesson activities that involve waiting a turn, there are, of course, certain sports that by their very nature and design can lead to high levels of inactivity. As such, acceptance of inactivity should be avoided. View the removal of inactivity as a challenge in the planning phase prior to a lesson. Creatively aim to include conditions that maximise all pupils' involvement. Practitioners must aim to avoid the Netball Goalkeeper and Goal-Shooter being stood inactive whilst play is at the other end of the court, or the fielder in a rounders or cricket lesson admirably watching the county player hit run after run whilst they stand in the outfield, potentially fielding a ball once every five minutes. The reality is that position-specific development is not going to take place in a lesson environment; this is an extra-curricular, or focus for a club training session. In the contexts provided above, your role is to develop a broader appreciation for the sports of netball and cricket, as opposed to a responsibility to develop goal shooters or wicket-keepers.

Consider opportunities for 'Active Bursts' or however you wish to brand them. Allow a student to select a movement or exercise that the entire group must perform on command, use your enthusiasm as a teacher to rev the group up for 30 seconds of star jumps in the middle of game-play sessions. Every time the ball goes out of play, a change of position or a skill challenge against the clock. Inject that energy and activity into lessons when it may not be immediately forthcoming, if the game were to be played in its natural environment. These strategies can prove invaluable if you are also competing against the elements. Teaching in a northern, coastal town, employing these strategies is a matter of survival!

Another effective thought process to consider when planning a lesson is to put yourself into that Y8 child's shoes in your lesson. Which aspects of PE did you enjoy the most? The parts where you were static, listening to a teacher laboriously go over the nuances of a particular skill, or did you enjoy the doing? Learning and developing whilst being active? Of course, the posing of this question is relatively rhetorical, so how can we avoid lessons being too 'stop, start'?

Essentially, once a lesson theme is introduced, the activity should be able to run, and run, especially in a games- or performance-based activity. As a PE teacher, try to circulate around a group and move on pairings or small groups without stopping the entire class. Drip feed in progressions as appropriate to avoid cognitive overload. Take time to step back and observe how pupils are working. When you stand back, are all of your pupils on task? Do any pupils need support? Do they need help moving out of their comfort or easy zone? Could you challenge them further by adding competition, or a condition that is going to keep them primarily active but also creates an environment for them to keep progressing? Equally, is a group becoming disengaged, as an activity may be too difficult or complex? If so, simplify the activity – take away any restrictive conditions to encourage the activity levels that are trying to be reached.

Whilst these strategies are essentially differentiation by task, pace and groupings, it receives a worthy mention within this chapter, as being able to differentiate in this way can maximise activity for all. Take a class of 28. Stopping 4 pupils to provide bespoke feedback or to add a progression ensures the other 24 pupils continue to be active. Swiftly circulating around each group of 4 can ensure that, whilst a small percentage of the group are briefly inactive, the vast majority are continuing to be on the move.

Finally, it is worth taking time to consider the bookends of PE lessons. These are the first and last 2-3 minutes of a lesson. As soon as pupils enter a sports hall, can they begin an independent warm-up? Basic skill practice? Is it essential that they wait patiently on a bench whilst the pupil that takes the longest to get changed enters the hall? Immediate activity can be a routine and an expectation that you instil in your pupils from the outset, and maintain in a range of teaching settings. If a lesson is taking place on an outdoor field space, several hundred metres away from the changing room, could pupils jog as a class to the working area? Could it be a challenge to see who can get their warm-up started first? At the end of a lesson, could pupils conduct a cool-down on the way back in from an outdoor learning space? Could it be a challenge to get back to the changing rooms as quickly as possible, if you've squeezed every drop of lesson time from your allocated 1hr? Instil high expectations linked to activity into your pupils, and their engagement and motivation will support you in your mission to hit those magical activity levels that underpin great PE lessons.

If a young person is moving, they are getting fitter, they are learning more about movement, their bodies, and how exercise can make them feel. If they are moving, they have an immediate focus, their engagement is higher, and low-level disruption is minimised. Creating that 'buzz', energy and excitement in the lesson will naturally drive up that activity without pupils realising how hard they are actually working! I implore you, get the activity levels high, and progress and engagement will go up, whilst your stress levels will go down!

Top 3 Takeaways!

1. **Record your next PE lesson.**
   Watch it back with your mentor or a colleague, and focus on the pupil's activity time. If activity levels are low, consider tweaks in lesson design to address this ahead of the next lesson.

2. **Observe an experienced colleague delivering a practical lesson.**
   Focus on the transitions between activities. Make notes of the strategies employed to keep pupils on task and active.

3. **Be prepared to step back and observe pupils during lessons.**
   Then, feedback to and challenge small groups within a class whilst the rest keep working.

Chapter Reflection

Phil Mathe, Director of Co-Curricular Provision at Brighton College, UAE and author of 'Happiness Factories'. *@PhilMathe79*

When Ben asked me to contribute to this section of his book, I took the time to reflect on what 'activity' means to me as a PE teacher and, more importantly, what 'activity' might mean to the pupils I teach on a weekly basis. I am a firm believer that context is key, and that PE should be designed and delivered in order to provide genuine meaning for the pupils it is being provided to. This means that many aspects of our provision are unique to our own environments. One size does not fit all, and the best PE programmes we see today ensure their pupils form the central point for any considerations made as to the type, style, volume, and meaning of anything they are provided with.

That said, there are a number of key aspects that most, if not all, PE teachers would agree must remain central to our subject's core purpose. Our subject is one of a handful that provides an opportunity for the development and maintenance of a positive attitude towards movement and activity. In a world dominated by sedentary lifestyles, and a seeping awareness of the challenges this will bring to our health and wellbeing (and indeed already is bringing), we are in a unique position to support the fight against the prevalence of acceptance culture around activity and movement. If you were to ask me what my key 'non-negotiable' is within PE today, it would definitely be the maintenance of activity levels. We deliver through 'doing' PE. We do this because we know that, in almost every situation, we can deliver through practical activity. If you were to ask any PE teacher trained within the past 20 years, they would almost universally tell you that almost every aspect of our core provision is delivered better within a practical situation. Practical is better, simple!

We know there are guidelines around physical activity levels within PE, and within wider school settings. We don't need to go into those here. We also know that, in the majority of settings, we are not meeting those activity level requirements. Beale et al. (2021) concluded their study into physical education levels in the UK with the depressing and yet not unexpected evidence that 'PE lessons were inactive compared to current guidance'. They recommend that, if we are to increase Physical activity, 'there is a need to introduce additional sessions of PE activity, focused on increasing physical activity'. Nothing groundbreaking here, but the stark reality of their research highlights that the issue is very much still with us. We must remember that one of our primary objectives when designing and delivering meaningful PE is to ensure our pupils are active, not just some of the time, or part of the time, but most of the time.

This doesn't mean we need to go back to our leadership teams and fight for more PE though. Whilst we would all love a 3 or 4 hour PE provision, the reality of most of our teaching environments does not sustain this. Therefore, we must work within our context. However much PE time your pupils get, we must maximise. Be clear in your thinking and planning. How and when are your pupils going to start being active; how are you going to maintain this activity; and how are you going to conserve this activity and movement, whilst also delivering teaching and learning? These are the questions we must ask ourselves during our planning process, and then refer back to in our delivery and then reflect on, post-lesson. You can tell when your pupils have been active – it's obvious. We don't need guidelines or timers to know when you've delivered a movement-rich lesson. Meaningful movement and purposeful activity are obviously going to be better, so challenge yourself to consistently maintain high levels within your lessons. Be the teacher who doesn't use queues or lines; be the teacher who models through movement; and be the teacher who maximises every valuable minute of their lessons. After all, why would we want to sit still? There is enough of that elsewhere in your school. Be the opposite, be the alternative, and be the lesson that makes the difference. Your pupils will thank you for it, today, tomorrow or at some point in their future.

B

Build up Your Resource Bank!

Carefully considering all the valuable resources around you and understanding how to store them can save you time, promote a positive work/life balance, and make you a more proficient practitioner.

It is never too early or too late to begin building up a resource bank linked to PE delivery. Now, people too commonly assume that a resource is something written down, usually looking pretty on laminated paper with some colour printing. Yes, this is obviously a resource type that can be used well to support the progress and development of learners within a lesson, but there are a multitude of other resource types that can be invaluable. We will take time to appreciate the range of resources shortly, but the most effective practitioners I have worked alongside have always banked and stored resources, ready to be withdrawn from their teacher toolkit when required. These practitioners also utilise an effective storage system, and know exactly where each resource is located. This filing method, somewhat metaphorical, can involve a tidy USB drive/OneDrive or DropBox folder, allowing these effective practitioners to be one step ahead through the time it can save them.

One resource that is often underappreciated is you. The only person to be present in every single lesson that you have delivered is you. Being able to reflect upon lessons can be a valuable resource. A colleague of mine that I have worked alongside for a number of years still uses a teaching journal. Now, as part of a PGCE, SCITT, or Teach First Programme, trainees are encouraged to reflect upon every lesson linked to a multitude of teaching standards or the 'Core Content Framework' (CCF), but for this colleague to continue to reflect so methodically, almost religiously, was incredibly impressive to see. The colleague simply used his journal to write brief bullet points on lessons he delivered. The journal was separated into the activities that made up our curriculum. An example from the journal might simply read, 'Football, 16th November, Y7 Boys, middle ability, passing, keep ball activity worked well, group engaged, differentiation by grouping and task, future lessons, enlarge working area by 5m'. By taking a few seconds to jot down these notes, the memories from this session are saved. The feelings that he had about the lesson, the engagement, the enjoyment, and any areas for development are stored. These can act as a parallel support mechanism for the part of the working memory that has also stored that lesson. We often think it is good enough to just think about these things, but the process of jotting them down helps capture information in our memories, as well as producing a record to revisit.

Fundamentally, trust your gut; you will be able to gauge a feeling from every lesson you deliver. You will be able to recognise triggers, such as pupils smiling, pushing themselves, and seeing skills beginning to develop. Noting down the names of pupils that smashed through learning objectives in a lesson, and equally those that struggled, is a vital starting point of reference ahead of future planning. The recognition of these triggers and pupils will help shape your future practice and delivery, but that recall process for you as a practitioner could be supported by a teaching journal or OneNote with a system filed class by class, for review ahead of future lessons.

Also, remember that pupils themselves are the most invaluable resource to a PE teacher. Utilising pupils to improve lesson delivery can be viewed from two perspectives. The pupil acts as a walking, talking Tripadvisor-Style provider of feedback, and as a versatile body of practical demonstrators! Pupils can provide the slo-mo, the full speed, the simplified and the complex demonstration that is relatable and supportive to the range of pupils participating in the lesson, and often is of a much higher quality than I am able to replicate, certainly as I move further away from my sporting prime every single day!

With regards to the Trip Advisor analogy, pupils are always brutally honest about PE lessons. Now, at times, this can lead to a practitioner needing to be thick skinned, as pupils can be critical of lessons. This is all part of the learning process for you as a practitioner. You quickly learn which feedback is worth reflecting upon, and which negative feedback is simply borne from the fact that the Y7 boys rugby group didn't get a chance to play a match at the end! When that pupil, who you know is usually a big fan of PE, does provide negative feedback, be resolute. It is sometimes not a nice feeling to hear that your biggest fan is being critical, but take a second to reflect on why they are voicing their negativity, include this in your evaluative thinking, and look to review your practice moving forward. This feedback process can also be formalised by encouraging pupils to use the 'what went well' (WWW) and 'even better if' (EBI) or Two Stars and Wish approaches often seen in primary schools. Providing this structure to the feedback process can bring about much richer and more useful feedback than off the cuff remarks about a lesson.

The contrast to this negative feedback is of course when a pupil or class provides positive feedback on a lesson or activity. There is no better feeling than hearing pupils react positively. I have been teaching for almost 15 years, and I still love the feeling that a pupil sharing their pleasure or joy for a PE lesson can give you as a teacher. Remember these moments. There are plenty of lows in teaching, plenty of occasions when your morale will be low (usually towards the end of November when it is minus 3, dark when you left for work, dark when you got back, and you are 4 weeks into an 8 week monster half term), so, from a mental health and well-being perspective, learn to appreciate the highs, the euphoria, and the 'buzz' that PE teaching can bring! In addition, remember to reflect and evaluate accordingly. Maybe even have a folder on the USB drive called 'Winning Lessons'; drop in the lesson plans from the days that went really well, then, when it comes to interviews, observations, etc, this resource will help you harness that positivity, improve and develop your mindset, and potentially even save you that valuable commodity in teaching…time!

Equally, pupil voice is such a powerful tool to utilise. This can be as structured or informal as you wish. It can take the form of a questionnaire, rich with qualitative and quantitative data, (pupils love to have their voice heard), in whichever form you choose. On a quicker and more simplistic level, factoring in a responsive plenary where pupils can provide immediate feedback can be useful -the classic thumbs up or down, perhaps? Or, right hand indicates enjoyment, left hand indicates learning. This will immediately open doors to further questioning (not simply challenging the lowest scoring pupil for enjoyment on how they could possibly have the audacity to question your lesson!) and it is an opportunity to extract that rich, live information from pupils that will positively impact your planning. Whilst observing lessons, or providing QA, I spend a large amount of time speaking to the pupils, ascertaining their appreciation for the lesson being delivered, but also their opinions or thoughts towards physical education in general. This can provide an ongoing feel for what each pupil's usual experiences are within the subject, not just how they feel on the day when the teacher knows they are being observed, so have hired the local circus and arranged for a pyrotechnics-based finale more suited to the X Factor!

To this end, pupil voice can be most effective when led by a colleague or leader within the school. This is where the most honest and useful data/feedback can be extracted and utilised to ultimately shape future practice. Our curriculum design was largely constructed following pupil voice feedback regarding attitudes and perceptions towards the activities, assessment, and approaches adopted by the department. The sample of pupils used was eclectic, and they were provided with an open, non-judgemental forum to share their views. Feedback was discussed at our departmental meetings with relevant actions linked to future delivery and curriculum structure put in place. This whole process develops cohesion between the department and pupils, both working towards the same end.

Colleagues within your departments and schools also provide an unrivalled resource depth for you to utilise. Without any disrespect intended, as a person starting out on your teaching career, your resource bank would probably be more appropriately titled your 'Resource Piggy Bank'. You've been saving for a bit, you are getting used to saving and filing away but a colleague that has been working for over a decade, their resource bank is like one of those bank vaults you see in the movies. Every day, every lesson, valuable information is deposited in there, ready to be spent as and when needed. That said, your new kid on the block fresh ideas might be just what a department needs. You can be the person to freshen up approaches and practices. If you have an idea or practice that you know is effective, share and collaborate.

Every PE teacher I have worked alongside has been forthcoming when I've asked them for their ideas, strategies, or thoughts regarding any aspect of the profession. This is mainly due to two reasons: firstly, PE teachers love to share lessons that have gone well or that they firmly believe in; secondly, PE teachers are used to being part of a team. They appreciate the importance of teamwork, and have all been through the same PE teaching circle of life themselves – they were once at the start of their careers, asking an elder PE statesman for their advice. This process has existed for generations, and will continue to exist for many more. We are blessed in that, commonly, PE teachers interact much more than other, more classroom-bound subject teachers. These greater opportunities for interaction are invaluable, and so much can be learnt through simple conversation between colleagues.

In addition to the experience and wisdom that colleagues can provide, they can also share strategies and ideas from their area of specialism. I have yet to meet a PE teacher that, whilst being a gold medal contender for the Decathlon or Heptathlon, was also a district gymnast, swimmer, dancer and tennis player. Excellence across multiple sporting areas is not expected, but an appreciation and a level of teaching proficiency across a curriculum is to be expected eventually. To help you in your quest to achieve this, pick the brains of colleagues regarding their strongest sporting areas. Firstly, and similarly to above, colleagues love to talk about their sporting passion but, secondly, they have experience of how to deliver these activities from the perspective of the pupil, considering that they themselves were a pupil, and probably a talented pupil at that. During my NQT year, I actively sought guidance on areas of the curriculum that were my weakest. Having grown up in a predominantly rugby league area, I had very little experience of rugby union. Thankfully, a colleague of mine had played union at a county level. I simply used to observe parts of his lessons, and went to fixtures to help me understand the nuances of alien concepts such as rucks, mauls, and contested scrums. The time invested during the earlier years of my career has provided me with a solid base of subject knowledge that has been of great benefit ever since.

Adding further to subject knowledge, be sure to withdraw as much broader 'teacher currency' from experienced colleagues' 'ATM' as possible. Observe how other members of the department communicate with pupils and each other: how do they quieten a group for whole class instruction; how do they calm a distressed pupil; how do they work restoratively with challenging pupils? The list of invaluable tips and tricks that can be learned by observation of colleagues is endless. Put time aside to shadow colleagues within PE, but also other subject areas, and be sure to make notes of your observations for future reference.

The more traditional resources of lesson plans, teaching aids, and task cards are also worth storing in a location that is easily accessible. In a similar thread to the teaching journal mentioned before, try to be organised, ensure that the USB drive (showing my age) or cloud-based saving function is tidy, separated by activity folders and into year groups so it can be utilised effectively as you need. In addition to activity-specific resources, create a contingency folder. This folder will act as your 'Plan B'. In PE teaching, there are so many ways across an academic year that your timetabled lesson might be disrupted. Inclement weather, staff absences, vaccinations, school photographs and examinations are the most regular culprits that can throw you from your intended plan with very little notice. Being able to access that wet weather lesson with a high level of immediacy will provide you with a sense of calm in a situation of panic brought about by that unprepared feeling. As you move through your career, this contingency document might evolve into a contingency folder. A single page with lesson titles and perhaps a couple of notes about lesson organisation can alleviate the stresses of being thrown off-course by an unexpected barrier to your planned lesson, and allow you to deliver successful lessons in situations of constraint and differing circumstances.

The importance of taking time to collate resources cannot be underestimated. Even though I used the ATM analogy earlier, this is slightly different. Your teaching bank balance never actually drops after a withdrawal, it continues to be topped up through the 'interest' that your teaching career will provide with every lesson, day, week, and term that you work through. Invest in building it up, but also applying it in flexible ways, as no two classes or situations are the same – such is the beauty, but also the challenge, of being a physical educator.

Top 3 Takeaways!

1. **Complete a resource audit.**
   Review your USB/One Drive: are there any topic or activity areas that have limited resources? If so, be proactive, research, use #EduTwitter and harvest fresh, usable resources to enhance your delivery.

2. **Build up your network.**
   Reach out and connect with PE teachers in your local area. Explore opportunities to get out and observe peers and take away their best practices to use in your context.

3. **Conduct a pupil voice following your next lesson.**
   5-10 minute chat with a range of pupils. It's a great way to build relationships, and pupils are often brilliant at providing honest feedback for you to take forward and implement in future lessons.

Chapter Reflection

Zeph Bennett. *@PEGeeksCorner*

Ben has taken a methodical approach to how resources look within PE, and ways any PE teacher can improve and develop their resources to aid their teaching in an increasingly complex and demanding secondary school environment post-covid.

The basic habit of note taking and reflecting on what went well in a journal is one of the most valuable lessons to be learned when trainee teachers move into full time teaching. The habit of reflection and responding to pupil feedback through simple questioning enables us to know instinctively what has worked, and what can be repeated successfully in the future. This invaluable information, as Ben highlights, must be recorded.

Ben explores the breadth of resources available to the PE teacher, from the pupil demonstrating a complex skill and the older colleague who has mastered what works within a physical activity, to the elite performer colleague who has the skill set in an activity we are not confident in. These are resources we can all tap into to ultimately improve our teaching competence.

Understanding that, as PE teachers, we are not experts in all sporting disciplines is important for new teachers to the profession to acknowledge, as it will form the basis of your own skill development in PE that continues throughout your teaching career. Teaching proficiency in a range of sporting activities, as Ben points out, takes time and practice. With teaching skills comes practice, awareness, and eventually proficiency.

Ben is quite right to focus on the metaphorical 'resource' that cannot be stored in a well-written journal or google drive, but evolves with observation and feedback from colleagues. The significance of picking up routines and classroom management tips used by experienced practitioners, and then developing them with your own teaching toolkit, is invaluable, and any experienced teacher will tell you that we are all still magpie-ing great ideas when we see them used successfully in the classroom or out on the playing fields.

This chapter also explores how PE teachers must develop a degree of adaptability, and the ability to change from a planned lesson when facilities or weather forces your hand. This experience is unique to the PE teacher, and one which requires an ace up your sleeve. Having a repertoire of wet weather or alternative lessons is very important for any PE teacher, and developing effective ones with a renewed focus on curriculum and the bigger picture is essential for all practitioners.

We can all learn something from how we develop and build our resources. The more effectively we do it, the more likely we are to continue to successfully improve our own teaching methodology.

C

Competition

*Every aspect of a lesson can include an element of competition. When you know your classes and pupils well, you can organise competition in a way that will engage all pupils with PE. After all, **life is competitive**, and self-improvement can be addictive!*

Imagine your own school days. You're back in Year 7, in the sports hall. You are bright red, sweating, the scores are tied, the PE teacher shouts those immortal words, 'Next Goal Wins!' The ball comes across to you, you're in space and bang, you've done it, you've scored the winning goal. You can all picture a moment like this. The sport might change, the setting might change, but you have all been part of a PE lesson with a similar finale, and it's probably one of these moments that got you hooked on PE in the first place...

This example of competition within the PE teaching profession transcends down to the importance of a prevalence of competition within our PE lessons, and an appreciation of competition for our young people. A person's life will have numerous situations where they will be in competition with another individual, team or themselves. The joy that winning can bring to a person, that sense of achievement, is an invaluable accelerator of intrinsic motivation within a young person. In addition, young people need to develop the ability to lose. Not every competition that people enter will result in victory. Everyone has suffered a defeat, and it is an important characteristic for a young person to be able to lose with dignity and humility whilst also developing that hunger within to want to win next time. This thread is vital within primary school children. Equipping our youngest pupils with the emotional capacity to experience adversity and defeat is an important characteristic. Teaching should recognise gracious winners and losers.

In order to prepare young people for the big, wide world, for employment, for their future sporting careers, I am a firm believer that competition should be incorporated into all physical education lessons. Now, I am aware that this will arguably be the most opinionated section of this book, and will certainly ruffle the feathers of those few that celebrate the usage of 'Participation Certificates', and sports tournaments where results aren't recorded, but I believe allowing young people to access competition is crucial. The skill of a practitioner in employing differentiation, conditions, and fundamentally building a relationship where you know your pupils, is what will ensure that competition is structured appropriately to engage everyone.

Competition levelling is crucial, as it ultimately underpins whether including competitive elements into your lessons will have the desired impact of increasing engagement. The ability-to-level competitions is something that becomes easier with experience, as you will quickly be able to see which conditions, challenges, games, and timings work with certain age groups, genders, and ability levels.

If a competitive element is woven into your lesson design, consider all pupils that are due to participate. How can competition be used skilfully to create that 'buzz' that good PE lessons have? Do you need to take time prior to the lesson to pick partners or teams that are going to be competing against each other? Do you need to consider scoring systems, conditions, rules, or positions that are going to ensure the engagement of the majority of pupils in the session? Often, a complacent practitioner will simply throw in a match towards the end of a lesson, but an outstanding practitioner will take time to consider the aspects mentioned above, whilst also weaving competition into many aspects of a lesson, even down to elements such as collecting cones, or who can gather back round the teacher the quickest.

A teaching style that I implore you to research is Sport Education: a model that involves dissemination of roles to all participants in a team, and encourages pupils to develop their leadership skills in a competitive environment. I have observed the model being implemented successfully from Key Stage 1 to Key Stage 5. The model can be applied to any sporting activity, and the tracking of points awarded for match wins, best warm-ups, match reports, fair play, and leadership qualities demonstrated allows lessons to be inclusive, and encourages pupils to experience a wider range of roles than in a normal lesson environment. The model also promotes applicable life skills. Pupils must self-manage, regulate emotion towards success and disappointment, whilst also developing an understanding of how to be an effective member of a team. We use the model year on year as part of our curriculum, and pupil voice always reflects favourably on it. The beauty of Sport Education is that you can modify and adapt the broader model to suit your context. We apply a point penalty to pupils not following our kit policy. Commonly, offenders early on in a term turn out to be the shining stars, religiously remembering their full kit and contributing to the success of a team. In my opinion, the power of Sport Education and competition is unrivalled.

As discussed, several times within this chapter, competition can lead to engagement during and within lessons, but it can also lead to a longer lasting motivation from a pupil. That motivation is often borne from one of two scenarios. The extrinsic motivation provided by a victory, or the intrinsic motivation that will hopefully be fostered if a pupil is defeated. This is where skilled practitioners are aware of the nature of their classes, individual pupils, and how the usage of tools such as verbal praise and reassurance can be crucial. Awareness of pupils will allow teachers to give feedback based on prior performance and self-improvement, as opposed to a complete ego-orientated comparison against others. Recognition of contextual effort, displays of sportsmanship, and encouragement of others through teacher- and peer-praise can all be incredibly powerful in shaping pupils' future behaviours.

A simple Player of the Match (POTM) or Most Valuable Player (MVP) award can be a powerful means of recognition for a young person and, if in a pocket-sized certificate form (any bigger and the likelihood of it being found in the letter/paper-based graveyard that is the bottom of a school bag several years later increases dramatically), this can be taken home to be celebrated further by parents or carers. This POTM/MVP awarding can be made even more powerful if the pupil receiving the accolade is chosen by other members of the class or the opposition. This simple peer assessment method can be incredibly motivating to a pupil to continue to push themselves in lessons and can often lead to a pupil taking a first step into extra-curricular sessions linked to that activity. As a practitioner, with experience, you will ascertain how best to include such a process in your lessons, or whether the POTM ceremony is best to be conducted by you, as the teacher, or by peers. With such awards ceremonies, make note of the recipients of each lesson to avoid the same pupils being recognised each week, and to ensure a fair spread of recognition across a class.

As intimated earlier, competition will obviously lead to several pupils experiencing defeat within lessons. On these occasions, the importance of skilful verbal communication from a teacher, supported by an empathetic approach, is crucial to ensure that a defeat does not result in resentment towards PE, but lights that fire in a young person's belly – that intrinsic motivation within them to demonstrate that 'Bouncebackability' Iain Dowie talked about in the early 2000s.

In addition to being in competition with a peer or another team, a pupil should be encouraged to be in competition with themselves. This is where a teacher will essentially use differentiation by outcome. This is another aspect of teaching that will develop with experience, and it is advised to utilise the specific subject knowledge expertise that a colleague could provide. Furthermore, taking time to research national averages for age groups and genders within activities can enable you to accurately set a pupil a target within a lesson, especially for those of higher ability.

Within games lessons, setting competitive personalised targets for pupils, such as completing a certain number of repetitions within a timeframe, can help create that PE lesson 'buzz'. Dribbling activities within basketball, football or hockey can have that injection of energy if a class is provided a Gold, Silver and Bronze medal standard that links to the number of successful completions of a dribbling circuit within 2 minutes. Pupils also enjoy setting and beating personal bests; build the opportunity for pupils to set new high scores, and all those fundamental aspects of a PE lesson such as energy, activity, and enjoyment will be prevalent to pupils, yourself as the practitioner, and any other observers.

A further competitive element, as I am sure you will be aware, is one of the most competitive job markets – that of securing a position as a full-time PE teacher within a school. And, one of the most competitive postgraduate courses is that of an ITT pathway within physical education. Such is the fantastic nature of this career path that it does prove popular at every level. Undergraduate and trainee teachers must consider what methods might allow them to beat their competition. How can they stand out from the crowd? Hopefully, following the conclusion of this book, the tips, ideas and guidance will enable you to become a candidate that is a perfect fit for an ITT provider, school, or college.

Competition, if correctly designed, applied, and rewarded can be one of the most impactful tools in a PE teacher's toolkit. Weave it into your lessons when you can, and appreciate the competitive world of PE teaching in its entirety!

Top 3 Takeaways!

1. **Research and observe performance levels linked to each key stage and year group.**
    Use these to accurately pitch competitive scenarios in lessons.

2. **Design awards for your lessons.**
    POTM, MVP, Spirit of PE awards, and use them to recognise and inspire.
    Make note of recipients and ensure a wide spread of winners across a term

3. **Appreciate the competitiveness of the PE teaching market.**
    Take ownership in making yourself a unique and unmissable proposition to prospective employers!

Chapter Reflection

Nick Shepherd. PE teacher and 2nd in Department based in Yorkshire, England.
@MrShepherdPE

This is a subject which has divided opinion during my time as a practitioner, the constant dilemma of whether to provide a 'participation' or 'competitive' ethos, in order to best support students within PE, is often a topic of heated debate.

Myself? I am firmly in the 'competition camp'. Within this chapter alone there is evidence and testimony which echoes my thoughts around how competition can be structured and developed in order to provide so many benefits for the students involved. But it is the craft of the teacher that is key to this competitive element being successful, driving the development of young people towards their long-term goals.

The phrase that really stands out for me is 'when you know your classes and pupils well...'. This is a mantra which I have held from day one, and is the number one piece of advice/ guidance that I received as a new teacher, and continue to pass on to anyone entering the profession.

Alongside taking the time to have conversations with students, get to know them as individuals – what creates that spark for them? This allows for competition to be made relevant, accessible and enjoyable.

The Sport Education model is one that I have utilised throughout my career, and will always continue to do so. It allows me to implement so many of the fundamentals of PE. The use of different roles for different students means that I can tailor their experience so that they not only feel part of a team, but that their contribution is recognised as one of the keys to potential success. Using roles such as coach, kit manager, analyst, and official also allows for a shift in focus away from the skill development/application, and highlights different ways in which people can be involved within sports. Hearing discussions in the changing room and at break/lunchtime around tactics, analysis and strategy is so gratifying.

We look to praise as much as possible, and utilise peer praise where teams select the POTM for either their own or another team. This is interspersed with my own praise that highlights effort, consistency, sportsmanship, attitude, etc. Recognising all contributions is key in creating that 'buzz' that good competition breeds...like no other.

Competition isn't just a mainstay on the field, pitch, track, or court...it is something that we all face throughout life. I often find myself emphasising this within the classroom to GCSE/BTEC/OCR cohorts – the fact that they are in competition for post-16 places, apprenticeships, and jobs. In my opinion, the implementation of competition within a theoretical setting has huge benefits, providing a wide-reaching, positive influence across the whole-school curriculum...and PE is at the forefront!

We are in a unique position to have a vehicle in 'competition' with which to overtly facilitate the development of so many life skills: planning, resilience, respect, communication, cooperation, evaluation, goal-setting (the list goes on). Use it well.

D
Do Not Become Disheartened!

There is no other subject area that will include so many setbacks. Be resilient, reflect effectively, and use any challenging experience to shape your delivery in the future.

Nothing infuriates me more than when the clichéd criticisms of the PE teaching profession are levelled at us. 'All you do is kick a ball around.' 'You don't have any marking though, do you?' 'Alright for you lot isn't it? Getting to be outside in the sun all day.' Do not get me started about this last one; I teach in the north east of England, we get about 5 days a year where the temperature gets above 12 degrees and, even then, we are greeted with 50mph winds!

I mean, do not get me wrong, I have a plethora of retorts ready if these clichés are thrown towards me, but I do think there is a lack of appreciation for the daily challenges that PE teachers face. Our subject is unique. Coping with the potential of 5 different teaching environments and 5 different activities in a 5-lesson day is the norm. The range of subject knowledge requirements is one of the broadest in the profession, and it is all these aspects that can lead to PE teachers becoming disheartened – the complexity of our job is, in my opinion, unrivalled.

PE lessons will go wrong, activities will not run as you had pictured in your mind, and activities that worked well with one class might not work well with another. You have 20-30+ young people in your lessons. Each of these young people approach a lesson with a different mindset. Some may have just been reprimanded from a different subject; some may be experiencing difficulties at home; some may be under the weather; some may have not slept last night. All these different potential barriers to engagement are out of your control, yet all of them are about to be mixed in a PE lesson context. When you put it like this, it is worth celebrating when a lesson goes well – some might consider it to be a minor miracle!

The point I am trying to make is that there are often a multitude of variables beyond your control that can impact the effectiveness of a lesson, or activity within a lesson. All these potential issues with pupils within lessons are challenging enough, never mind the torrential rain shower that wasn't forecast, the dog that ran onto the fields midway through a bowling demonstration, or the fire drill you were not aware of that was conveniently placed just after your year 7's had finished their warm-up!

The key element of advice to consider here is to avoid using these variables as an excuse (although, if a stray dog does run onto your field, it is one of those moments where I do think you can use this as an excuse as your Year 8's go wild!), but to use each unique scenario that can negatively impact a lesson as an opportunity to reflect. Appreciate that not all lessons will be absolute showstoppers, and take time to learn from moments of PE teaching adversity, and use them to shape lesson design in the future.

As PE teachers become more experienced, solid practitioners, one of the most admirable and crucial qualities is to be able to adapt and think on your feet. Some activities may need curtailing, while some might need extending until a concept or key skill is grasped; this might mean pupils don't get to measure their jump, or get into a conditioned game, but the overall rationale from you as a practitioner is justified. How does this link into a chapter on not becoming disheartened? Essentially, if a lesson isn't working, do not simply accept this and blame a variable or make an excuse such as, 'the pupils were hyper today' – don't give up mid-lesson. Instead, take a moment to consider what could be done to improve the overall lesson experience through scanning and observing pupil attitudes towards learning and engagement. Then, make adaptations swiftly and, depending on your relationship with the class, have the confidence to share your reasoning for deviating from the plan to the pupils. They will be understanding, and will also be grateful if a subtle change to an activity leads to more engagement and activity time.

It can be damaging for morale when elements of lessons do not go to plan, but it can be soul destroying when things don't go to plan during a lesson observation. Lesson observations can be a contentious discussion point, and one that I could debate at length. Personally, when I observe a lesson of a member of our department, or of a trainee teacher, I try to apply as much context to the observation as possible. Elements such as level of experience, subject specialisms, variables as mentioned earlier, and whether the member of staff has played it safe or been bold and tried something different or new are all mentally noted prior and during observations. Unfortunately, not all lesson observers apply these contextual considerations, perhaps they are unable to appreciate them, especially if they are observing the lesson outside of their specialism, or they do not appreciate aspects of the lessons that are specific to the school, such as the behaviour and general attitudes towards PE of the pupils in the lesson.

If you feel an observer is unable to apply the required context, be sure to explain the reasoning that underpinned the overall design and delivery of the lesson. Do not feel afraid to share this. Furthermore, be sure to outline the bigger picture of a lesson within a unit of work, or a particular phase of the curriculum. This bigger picture, if shared prior to delivery, can help an observer appreciate elements of a lesson and, if shared following a lesson, can, as mentioned earlier, help an observer to understand your thinking around design. An experienced observer should provide you with an opportunity to share your views on the lesson as part of your overall reflection process, but sharing your perception of the lesson context can be valuable for the observer to hear, so be prepared to discuss this during lesson feedback.

Throughout a teaching career, lessons will be observed. From Initial Teacher Training, all the way up to senior leadership, people will observe lessons and share their opinion of your craft. Being an effective practitioner is about absorbing critique given, and applying any guidance or advice given to future lesson delivery and practice. To apply critique or new ideas into future teaching can be challenging; teachers are often creatures of habit. Remember, just because 'you've always done it like that' does not mean that your way is the best way. Display humility and consciously act upon feedback in day-to-day practice, not just during the next observation cycle, and this positive practice will become established.

A further aspect of the journey to becoming a PE teacher that can be disheartening is the competitive nature of the profession, as discussed in the previous chapter. At each juncture, you will be in competition with many people for work experience opportunities, further education courses, PGCE or SCITT course places, and job roles within a school. There will be setbacks – this is only natural when so many people have the ambition to work in such a fantastic profession. If you are unsuccessful for a particular role, try not to be too disheartened; display resilience, request feedback, act upon it, and continue to move forward. If the feedback is linked to the interview, request a mock interview with a friend, colleague, or mentor. If the feedback focuses on the lesson itself, conduct a self-review and be proactive in responding to the feedback provided by the school or PGCE Leader. If the feedback was critical of the covering letter provided, ask a mentor or colleague to proofread it and provide specific feedback – have you sold yourself enough?

Have you undersold yourself? Fundamentally, take stock, reflect honestly and positively, and continue to stride forward as commonly, you may have done everything in your power during the application process, but might not have just been the right fit for that school at that time.

Take solace in the fact that there will be future opportunities that arise within physical education. PE teachers often make great leaders. As such, it is common that main-scale PE teachers progress and take up positions of middle and senior leadership within schools – this can lead to more PE teaching positions becoming available. Ultimately, the world of education moves quickly and, remember, the absolutely perfect school rarely exists. Be prepared to make compromises around elements like travel, location, demographics, and pre-conceptions as you will often be able to adapt and prosper once in employment.

The Post Graduate Certificate of Education (PGCE) or School Centred Initial Teacher Training (SCITT) year will be the most challenging of your life. You will be exhausted. You will be emotional. I am sure you will be disheartened and, potentially, even begin asking yourself whether this career is the right one for you. At these times of your lowest ebb, dig deep and keep moving towards that finish line. Actively address a healthy work-life balance. Your well-being is crucial. Access your support network. Be resilient, take feedback on board, professionally and positively, and I can wholeheartedly reassure you that it will all be worth it in the end.

Top 3 Takeaways!

1. **During lesson observation feedback, be honest with the observer and your mentor.**
   The process is most effective for your development if discussions are open with both voices heard.

2. **Be sure to talk to mentors, colleagues and friends during the tougher times.**
   This support network is crucial.

3. **Lessons do not always go to plan.**
   Reflect, take stock and move forward. You've got this.

Chapter Reflection

Steve Johns - Head of Boys PE, SCITT and ECT Mentor. *@SteveDJohns*

It's true – PE teachers are some of the most versatile, adaptable, creative, and solution-focused practitioners in any line of work. It's the only subject where, in a five-lesson day, you could teach in the sports hall, a classroom, a computer room, the field, and the fitness suite, all between doing duties and after school clubs in different parts of the school. This has obvious transferable benefits to leadership roles and progression opportunities, so dive in and enjoy it!

In my teaching experience, I have worked with some truly resilient colleagues who have had every challenge thrown at them: from dreadful weather to facility changes to student emergencies, and that's before we even get to in-lesson challenges that we continually strive to overcome. I consider the main in-lesson challenges to be differentiation, inclusion, demonstrations, activity levels, interventions, behaviour management, positive relationships, non-doers, health and safety, and assessment, among many others. Managing these variables in an open and dynamic setting, with active and excited students, is what we live for and is why we chose this profession. Let's relish the challenge and get comfortable with the fact that it is often impossible to manage everything at once.

However, effective planning and preparation will enable all of the above to become easier – it doesn't always just 'happen'.

Do not be disheartened. I have had observations that I have planned to the hilt and they have bombed. I have also had lessons with no expectation and minimal planning that achieved fantastic outcomes, full engagement, and a genuine love of our subject from the students. Have faith in this as a process. It's hard not to think in absolutes, but be realistic, and don't expect every lesson to be outstanding (or what you deem outstanding). Prioritise, prepare, execute as well as possible, and you can have peace of mind that you are doing your best.

In terms of interviews, I've had many throughout my career – my top tip is to remember that, on the day, you are (internally) interviewing the school as much as they are interviewing you. You will know what you are looking for. You need to find this out through asking planned questions throughout an interview day to staff, students, and interview panels when you can.

A thought to leave you with is this: please remember that you must control the controllable. Do not underestimate the impact that effective planning, preparation and assessment can have on your lessons, for your confidence, if nothing else. Work as a team player to develop and share resources in your department and in the PE community. On a similar note, don't sweat the small stuff. Students say things which might hurt. Lessons don't go to plan. You will need support at times. Ask for help and don't be too proud to share concerns, but don't let things you can't control affect your state of mind. We are very lucky to be in this profession, and I wish you a fantastic career.

E

Early Bird Gets the Worm!

Buying yourself valuable time throughout a busy working day can be incredibly useful in helping you manage your workload, and support you in maintaining positive mental health and well-being in the workplace.

Teaching is one of those professions where you always feel bereft of time. The role of a teacher is often coupled with the role of a form tutor, a team manager, a team player, and not to mention the much more crucial roles of being a son or daughter, boyfriend or girlfriend, husband, wife and father or mother. As such, there is the necessity to buy yourself as much time as possible.

One of the most invaluable habits and routines that I have worked hard to maintain throughout my career is to get into work as early as possible. This hasn't been easy, and obviously the added responsibilities of parenthood has made this even more challenging (and at this point I must thank my wife once again for her unwavering support), but I religiously get settled at my desk at 7am every morning. This time in the morning is precious. There aren't the hustle and bustle and distractions of the mad 8.30am rush, with everyone starting to prepare their day. It provides time to conduct some important administration in the form of emails arranging fixtures, replying to parents, management of data, whilst also providing an opportunity to prepare lesson materials, set up and organise resources, and ensure that any resources required for lessons later in the day are accessible and not going to cost me that valuable commodity of time as the day progresses.

Now, 7am to some may seem extreme, but I cannot recommend highly enough getting into work and allowing yourself to settle, sticking the kettle on, and having a composed and controlled start to the working day. Too often, I have witnessed colleagues rushing into work just before 8.30am and they continue to play catch-up until 3pm, and then commonly work until late just to keep in front. Those jobs that my colleagues spend until 6pm completing in the evening are jobs that I have completed by 8am. The positive work/life balance this routine provides, along with, that word again, 'time' that it frees up, fundamentally transcends into the quality of lesson that a practitioner can deliver.

I must stress at this point that this is a strategy that has worked for me with my circumstances. I appreciate that everyone's circumstances differ, but I must recommend that you take a moment to reflect on any habitual changes or tweaks that you could apply to buy yourself that valuable extra time. Procrastination is particularly dangerous. The world feels a better place with tasks sitting in the done pile as opposed to the to-do list. I appreciate that this is easy enough advice to give, but very challenging to apply. This said, give it a go; proactively approach tasks whilst preserving your well-being.

With more disposable time, a practitioner is able to focus on the nuances of a lesson, the targeted questioning that is to be deployed, and the groupings that will support differentiation, as opposed to chasing their tail and experiencing the frustrations that being unprepared can lead to, such as the cones not being available, someone needing the sports hall, the bibs not being where they should be, and the basketballs not being pumped up. All these possible barriers to lesson delivery are avoided by that early bird who was in with time to spare, and had the opportunity to check all of the minor elements of a lesson that could have larger consequences to delivery.

The next benefit of being early and prepared may seem as common as a unicorn sighting but, if you do have the opportunity, getting out prior to a lesson and setting up balls, cones, bibs, and tape measures, in the sports hall, MUGA, or field can just keep you that one step ahead for the forthcoming lesson. Being able to set lessons up fully or partially prior to their start time can also encourage immediate activity for pupils and get a lesson closer to those golden activity level targets that outstanding practitioners set themselves. In a basketball or netball lesson, simply having the balls ready for when the group arrives can mean that the fastest to get changed can begin shooting (which is what pupils immediately want to do anyway) whilst they wait for those that take longer to get ready. Another example is having simple cone ladders set out so that students can begin to perform basic SAQ exercises right at the start of a lesson. Covering these fundamental movements can help provide a higher foundation of quality for pupils that will, over time (routinely included in lessons across a term or even year), begin to manifest itself in the performance of other sport-specific movement skills, such as dribbling within invasion games, or court movement in net/wall games. Even simply having the lesson objectives and outcomes pre-written on the board can save precious time.

Moving away for a moment from lesson delivery, once you begin to appreciate the benefits of an early start and being punctual, you will begin to apply this philosophy to all aspects of your working day. Take Parents' Evenings, for example. At Parents' Evenings, you have a limited timeframe to further instil that element of trust that a parent places in you as their child's teacher. This sense of trust from a parent can be consolidated further, if you as the teacher are prepared with the required data, evidence, and discussion points that will allow an appointment to flow. Take time on the morning of a Parents' Evening to prepare such materials so that it does not become a rushed job in the hour between the end of the school day and the commencement of the appointments. Being able to give yourself a break at the end of the day can also be invaluable in sustaining energy levels throughout the gruelling endurance test that is a Parents' Evening!

The theme of this chapter is starting to become blatantly obvious but, once again, being early and prepared will help you when it comes to meetings. Now – sadly, some might say – as I have progressed through my career, I have found more and more meetings cluttering up my weekly schedule. But even in the infancy of my career, I had to attend meetings on a regular basis with people such as my NQT mentor, year leaders, departmental leaders, and individual parents' meetings – all of these were made easier for myself by being early and prepared. These qualities help to create and embed a positive impression and message about yourself as a professional person. They also help build confidence and trust, which can be crucial when working with parents and colleagues.

While we are talking about meetings, being prepared often consists of proving that you have taken the time to research and prepare material that is going to be discussed. If you have materials to share, ensure enough copies are printed out, that the content is correct, and presented in a manner that represents you as a professional. Furthermore, arrive at meetings with the capacity to take notes. This creates the perception that you are willing to take information away from the meeting and, most importantly, implement actions arising from the meeting.

Often inextricably linked to a meeting will be a deadline. This is where personal organisation is crucial. A number of colleagues that I have worked with over the years have used 'To-Do Lists' effectively to ensure deadlines are not missed. They also rank their to-do lists by priority in terms of importance, but also against the imminence of the deadline applied to the task. Also, 'red-flagging' or organising emails into 'Requires Action' folders is strongly recommended. This will provide a mental reminder of work needing to be completed, but also provide a great sense of accomplishment once a task is completed meaning that an email or action can be removed from the mental and/or email 'To-Do' folder. Naturally, however, not every deadline will be met; I certainly have not hit every deadline set during my career, but I do try to communicate this with line management and colleagues well in advance. Reaching out to colleagues for support ahead of tight deadlines is advised and, in my experience, teaching colleagues are good at offering that compassion towards deadlines, but only if they are kept in the loop regarding progress towards hitting a deadline. This approach is much more highly recommended than the 'burying your head in the sand' approach – this never ends well.

There are also some tasks within a working day that have no official 'deadline' attached to them, but are once again worthwhile to approach with an early bird attitude. Namely, requests from parents to return contact are always good ones to get out of the way early. Commonly, these can be quick (though for every 5 quick parental phone calls, there will always be that phone call that takes an hour) and can be dealt with swiftly so as not to hinder the progress of a child or give you longer term issues to deal with as the practitioner. Furthermore, a swift reply to a parent can be a great way to further develop their confidence and trust in you as a teacher.

Unofficial deadlines can often be presented to you by a colleague; in teaching, these can be by email after a meeting, or in passing in a corridor in between lessons. Returning these deadlines early and efficiently (with the required level of depth and quality) can once again build trust and confidence from colleagues in your ability to work under pressure in a school environment. Displaying this ability to colleagues of seniority can also be particularly useful when it comes to future career progression opportunities.

Punctuality in all aspects of teaching is a revered quality and viewed positively by colleagues, line managers, parents, and pupils. The benefits of approaching your working day with punctuality will quickly become recognisable, and you will also soon find them becoming habitual, which can only positively influence your effectiveness as a physical education teacher.

Top 3 Takeaways!

1. **Set your alarm 10 minutes earlier than usual for your next working day.**
   Try it – the additional calm it will bring will feel amazing!

2. **Before leaving school, ensure you are ready for tomorrow.**

3. **Challenge yourself to hit your next 3 deadlines as early as possible.**

Chapter Reflection

Will Swaithes. *@WillSwaithes*

I feel privileged to have taught physical education in a number of secondary schools since 2001, and now as a teacher educator. Since 2006, I have been lucky enough to spend time in a range of schools each year. First as an Advanced Skills Teacher deployed across Nottinghamshire, and then as a Specialist Leader of Education. I continue to lead that network of 20 PE subject leaders, but then, as Head of PE and Achievement for Youth Sport Trust, I had the insight and ability to influence PE policy and practise nationally that I am incredibly grateful for. If you haven't yet come across the Youth Sport Trust, then they need to go on your 'must follow' list, along with all the great contributors to this book, and I am proud to say I still do a lot with them. I have been mentoring trainee teachers since 2005, and love the fact I now lead a secondary PGCE PE programme at Birmingham City University. I also contribute regularly to Initial Teacher Education programmes at Loughborough and Buckingham universities, whilst squeezing our own consultancy work (www.PEScholar.com) in around the edges. As such, I have visited over 30 schools and engaged with hundreds of PE teachers in the last 12 months alone. From all those opportunities for insight, I have two main messages to share:

No two school contexts are the same. In fact, no two classes are the same, and even the same class is rarely the same on two different days (especially if the wind is blowing), so make sure you find a school that suits you AND be ready to observe then adapt during every lesson.

Life as a teacher is busy. Life as a physical education teacher can be beyond hectic. You will never teach the perfect lesson, and there is always more that can be done, BUT it is the most rewarding career. So, make sure you take care of yourself and remember to invest time in the things you love (like sport, your fitness, friends, and family) if you want to stand a hope of taking care of the students in your school. Also, build a habit of seizing the day.

Seizing the day is exactly the message you should be taking from this chapter. If you don't believe Ben or I about how crucial this is, then perhaps you should listen to Eddie Jones, and so many other successful leaders who swear by it. The 5am club by Robin Sharma is one of my favourite books, and they have a great Instagram page with top tips. I also like the idea of 'Eat That Frog' (Brian Tracey), whereby you tackle the most challenging task of your day first and don't allow yourself to procrastinate over it. If you are training to teach, that may be an assignment, or maybe it's planning a particular lesson that you are not very familiar with. If you can break the back of that AND get some exercise in before the school day really starts, then you will really feel the springboard effect on the rest of your day. To do well, you must be well and, consequently, if you can start every day by conquering an important task and doing something for you, then I am confident a great day will follow.

This chapter also covers the importance of being present in meetings; find ways to contribute to help you engage, but also to ensure you take something from every opportunity. It is important not to fall into the trap of counting down to half term to get a rest. Build some rest and recovery into every week, and be okay about not being the first to respond to emails, or leaving school on the bell once a week. Thanks for reading, and enjoy the rest of this survival handbook.

F

Future-Focused

Being proactive and anticipating the future in your career is thoroughly recommended. It can keep you current, relevant, and fresh. This will make you an invaluable member of any team, with an energy and drive to be original and ahead of the curve.

The most ambitious and successful people employed within education work hard in the present, but always keep one eye on the future. They have an ability to forward plan on a daily, weekly, and termly basis, to remain in control of their lessons and at the absolute pinnacle of their profession. This control that they maintain across all aspects of their working lives will transcend into quality. Completing tasks and delivering lessons of high quality becomes impossible to ignore by Senior Leadership within a school. Often, it is these individuals that receive consideration when it comes to promotion opportunities. These individuals will also be acutely aware that this future-focused approach to their work is due to their ambitious nature to progress through teaching and leadership positions within education. Personally, I used my ability for public speaking to put myself forward to deliver assemblies to whole year groups. These were often observed by the senior colleagues, and gave me the opportunity to showcase my confidence in addressing large groups, a key attribute for future leadership roles that, in all honesty, I already had half an eye on, even in the early stages of my career.

As we discuss the importance of actively considering your future within the profession, there will be aspects that apply to you, and there will be aspects discussed that you have already moved through at your current career stage. As such, this chapter will hopefully provide you with food for thought moving forward, or give you an opportunity to reflect on earlier stages in your career.

As you will be aware, and as previously discussed within this book, the PE teaching job market is one of the most competitive within education. If you are taking the time to read this book, you are either already lucky enough to be employed in an amazing role within teaching, or it is something you would like to do in the future. Having worked closely with several ITT providers, I know they are looking for graduates who are committed, but also unique. You must consider what will make you stand out from a very large crowd. My advice would be to conduct a personal audit at the start of your journey to becoming a PE Teacher (if this journey is already underway, do not worry, taking stock to reflect and conducting a skills audit is always a good idea!).

Firstly, consider your experience within different contexts. Are there any elements of education where your experience is limited? It could be that you have little or no Key Stage 5 experience; if this is the case, could you volunteer your services at a Sixth Form Provider/Post 16 Provider? The same can apply if you have limited GCSE PE or BTEC Sport experience. You may have limited opportunities on a timetable to teach girls or boys, or have few opportunities to work with SEND. Equally, you may have limited experience within primary PE. In the time period building up to my teacher training year, I actively volunteered to support PE delivery at the local primary school. This gave me an appreciation of the differences between key stages, but also experience of the fundamentals of practical activity delivery. Do not wait to be told that you lack experience within one of these areas during feedback from a job or course application that was unsuccessful – be proactive and address.

Education providers are often accommodating to people requesting experience placements. My advice during placement, especially if on an undergraduate or volunteer-based placement, is to display initiative, be positive, and be willing to take direction professionally. Every PE department loves a tidy store cupboard, and going in to give it a tidy of your own accord will always be received favourably! Gestures such as these are an opportunity for you to sell yourself as an enthusiastic person who has a real desire to work in the profession. Yes, some tasks may be mundane, but approach them with a willingness that illustrates your enthusiasm and commitment to the cause. The PE network is often referred to as a Village. Everyone knows everyone. Taking that time to get your face out there and recognised at fixtures and local events will be beneficial in the future. If you put in a real shift during an experience placement, this can only positively enhance your reputation and, in future months or years, it could lead to a full-time teaching position.

In addition, whilst on teaching practice, or an earlier period of work experience, be open with your mentor. The whole mentoring process is more beneficial for both parties if an open and honest forum is created. When mentees or people on placement claim to 'know it all', this can be very detrimental to the process and inhibit the progression and development of a trainee or young person on placement. Share your vulnerabilities, display humility, and explain areas in which you lack experience. This will enable the placement process to be more bespoke to your development. Yes, receiving praise for a solid lesson within your subject knowledge area of strength may feel nice in the short-term, but imagine the sense of euphoria you will feel if you step out of your comfort zone to teach a solid lesson in an area of weakness, following a period of dedicated research, observation, and application. Taking time at the start of a placement to explain exactly what you would like to get out of the process will help guide the overall experience for you, and allow the mentor to understand you more as a person willing to develop into a well-rounded PE practitioner. My biggest advice is not to try to hide your weakest areas. Instead, flag them up early and invite support to improve competence and confidence. A SWOT analysis conducted alongside a mentor is a worthwhile exercise that will be beneficial to your overall development.

During my teaching practice placements, I vividly remember meeting with a mentor to discuss adjustment to my teaching timetable after only 3 weeks of delivering lessons on my own. The mentor was very complimentary of my performance to date, which was obviously pleasing to hear, but I sensed the point he was trying to make. The activity areas of delivery for those first 3 weeks were football, basketball and netball. All of which ranked highly on my confidence audit, even in the infancy of my teaching career. I wasn't being stretched or challenged in respect of delivering out of my comfort zone, and with regards to subject knowledge familiarity. At first, I was reticent at giving up a golden ticket to hitting my teaching standards and progressing through my PGCE but, deep down, I knew that for my own development, to make me a well-rounded, employable proposition to schools in the future, I would have to take the plunge. The result was a newly constructed timetable that consisted of rugby union, gymnastics and dance. I reflect back on this meeting regularly and am grateful to this day that my mentor had the vision to appreciate that, for my future career readiness, I was ready to be pushed and challenged.

Following the initial audit on phases or types of educational settings, next, consider subject knowledge areas as part of your personal audit. Research the PE curriculum from a local school or within the school in which you are currently employed, and rank your confidence levels delivering each activity area from the curriculum. For the lower scoring areas, be proactive! A weak practitioner will become accepting of an area of weakness. I have worked with colleagues that simply state, 'I don't teach _____' or, 'I know enough to get by'. Is this approach fair on your pupils? I think not. A colleague of mine was tasked with leading on girls' football, despite this not being a particular area of expertise. Instead of shying away or moaning, she enrolled at a local football club and ended up

WANNA TEACH PE?

thoroughly enjoying the experience whilst improving her activity knowledge along the way! In addition, National Governing Bodies offer coaching awards at Level 1 that will give you a grounding and understanding within a weak activity area. Furthermore, there are now a multitude of online resources available for you to deepen your knowledge. YouTube, AfPE website, Youth Sports Trust, and a Twitter account closely linked to this publication are all accessible for you to take the time to deepen subject knowledge, but to also try something new.

Displaying your well-rounded subject knowledge is crucial at many different career stages. ITT or PGCE providers welcome candidates that have a range of coaching qualifications. Remember, however, that you are entering the profession to deliver high quality teaching and learning through a diverse and inclusive physical education curriculum, not just to deliver football, rugby or netball sessions. You are an educator, tasked with delivering a broad curriculum that is going to prepare pupils for lifelong physical activity – you are not a single sports coach. In addition to ITT, having a breadth of subject knowledge is very appealing to Heads of PE when it comes to deciding on a candidate for an NQT or Main-Scale PE teacher. I can speak from first-hand experience when I say that Heads of PE will be looking for someone to come in and deliver all activities on a PE curriculum as a minimum requirement. Heads of PE are also looking for candidates that can provide that little bit extra, or point of difference to the members of staff that already work within a department. Of all the recent appointments I have made for our department, each member of staff has provided additionality to the current offer. From cheerleading, golf and Gaelic football, appointed teachers have supported the growth of our department with their points of difference. Our curriculum is quite non-traditional with handball, tchoukball, kabaddi, capoeira, free-running and American football all covered during a year. Having a non-traditional activity in your teaching arsenal is fully recommended. Take control of your future and make yourself as employable as possible by making yourself as appealing as possible to prospective employers.

Keeping with the Head of PE thread, keep the future in your thoughts every day. Where do you see yourself in 5 or 15 years? If you wish to stay within the subject, take time to physically note down and record the work of a head of department, the decisions they make, the strategies they deploy. Also, do not be afraid to tell a head of department that you feel you may wish to take this career route in the future. A strong head of department will not see this as a threat but will be empowered by the support you display by buying into the shared vision for PE excellence within a school.

048

Taking all of the above into account, I am keen to stress that your career is not a race. It is not a comparison against peers at other schools and the promotions they might have been granted. The PE teaching craft takes time to refine, there is no rush to climb the career ladder. Often, stars will align when the time is right. I have seen first-hand a number of colleagues race up the ladder to positions of middle leadership at relatively early stages of their careers, and burn out/lose faith in the profession soon after. PE teaching is an incredible role to fulfil that can have such a powerful impact on pupils, there is no rush to dilute your focus away from teaching through extra responsibilities and roles that take you away from your core purpose and values.

By the same token, if there is another career path you are interested in, go and speak to the incumbent or specialist currently working in your school. Ask if you can meet with them or shadow them for a day, or take on a lead role for an element of PE. This is also worthwhile practice when it comes to applying for a middle leadership role. It shows willingness and an ownership for your own professional development and that can only be looked upon favourably by an employer. Fundamentally, however, experience in alternative roles or areas can provide perspective to your PE teaching, along with an added appreciation for the wider school context.

Essentially, the thread of this chapter has been for you to take control of your own future but it is not a race. Being a PE teacher is a brilliant and long career; enjoy every phase and moment, whilst keeping an eye and thought on the future. Be honest and be proactive when it comes to seeking the support you need to become a better PE teacher, and a more attractive proposition to an employer. You can always do more, learn more, research more, absorb more and become that missing piece of the jigsaw to a school or PE department through your relentless drive to become a more informed, well-rounded practitioner within physical education.

Top 3 Takeaways!

1. **Broaden your subject knowledge.**
   Challenge yourself to develop and deepen your understanding of a new activity area and concept, then have the bravery to deliver this to a class in the near future.

2. **Volunteer your services out of the PE bubble.**
   Broaden your outreach and knowledge by involving yourself in activities and projects led by other subject areas.

3. **Keep a log of all courses, professional developments.**
   Qualifications and experiences can be used to showcase you in future job applications.

Chapter Reflection

Lee Sullivan, Head of PE, South East England, Author of 'Is PE in Crisis?'
@Lee_Sullivan85

Following over ten years of teaching PE, I grew frustrated at just how little impact our sport-driven, technique-focused and performance-obsessed PE curriculum was having on a large proportion of students. Those students that considered themselves 'sporty' continued to thrive in lessons, turn up to extra-curricular clubs and engage, whilst the remaining students were being put off physical activity, potentially for life. Inadvertently, we were doing more harm than good. Following extensive research, conversations with many other physical educators, and numerous hours spent reflecting, I realised that the future of PE could in fact be very different. One goal for all physical educators should be to nurture physical literacy by providing positive and meaningful PE experiences for every child. I wanted to ignite change, start conversations and inspire teachers to meet this aim; therefore, I wrote 'Is PE in Crisis? Leading Meaningful Change in Physical Education'. The aim of this book was to bridge the gap between research and practice, share my vision, and offer a solution-focused approach to the current issues facing our subject.

'Wanna Teach PE?' is supporting people like you to step into your careers and thrive as physical educators. You are the future of physical education! However, I want to start off by talking about the present, your present, in the hope that by doing that it might better inform your future direction of travel. Take a moment to consider why you have decided to become a PE teacher. Very few people can articulate their 'why'. It is your cause or belief: why you do what you do. Ask yourself, 'why do you get out of bed every morning? And why should anyone care?' (Sinek, 2011, p. 39). If you are able to articulate your why, as a leader you can make more informed decisions, inspire others to join you on your mission, and have a better chance of realising your vision for PE. Always reflect on whether your current practice meets your 'why', and the 'why' of those in your care. If not, then it might be time to seek meaningful change.

This chapter talks clearly about creating a positive future for yourselves through continually learning, taking risks, volunteering, and honing your craft. I want to echo the point Ben makes regarding there being no rush to move up the ladder. Take the time to work on your teaching: plan and deliver outstanding lessons, develop your subject knowledge, understand the needs of your students, and ultimately leave PE in a better place than you found it. I highly recommend taking the time to read and listen to the work of Margaret Whitehead and Liz Durden-Myers around physical literacy, and Scott Kretchmar about meaningful PE (just for starters). If we are being future-focused, it is very difficult to comprehend the consequences, positive or negative, our lessons might have for years to come. With this in mind, it is also important to consider the futures of the young people you teach. The evidence is clear – if a child has negative experiences in PE, they are less likely to engage in physical activity in later life. Never underestimate the role we play in developing the relationship our students have with PE, physical activity, and sport.

For me, the key takeaways from this chapter are to seek continual development and be proactive when considering career progression. I have always been inspired by the innovators within our profession. Those that continue to read, listen and reflect. These leaders are not interested in delivering something just because that's how it's always been done, they want to leave a legacy – one that meets the needs of every student, improves physical and mental well-being, nurtures physical literacy, and genuinely prepares students for a physically active life. What will be your PE legacy?

G

Get to Know Your Pupils

Making a concerted effort to engage and interact with pupils can be incredibly powerful in empowering young people to share in your love of sport and physical activity. You have to share that you care before pupils care how much you know. Relationships are 95% of everything and, remember, in some young people's lives, you might be the only person that does show an interest…

If you were to take a moment to consider your own friendship group, I am going to guess that there will be commonalities when it comes to shared interests. Now, in the instance of a PE teacher and pupil, it is not a friendship that is looking to be developed, but the virtues are the same. For a pupil, being able to share a common interest with a PE teacher can help develop a positivity towards the teacher, which will resonate in an increased effort and respect during lessons. Taking time to ask if a pupil watched the netball, Olympics or rugby at the weekend, or indeed if they had a sports fixture themselves, can harness a perception of mutual respect, and lead to increased engagement within a lesson.

This development of mutual respect can be at its most powerful to you as a practitioner when working with a particularly challenging class with regards to behaviour and/or engagement. Taking time when on corridor or break duty to converse with young people about their lives or interests, sporting or not, will show that you really care, and this can be incredibly important, especially to the most vulnerable.

Take time to reward positive behaviours demonstrated in lessons, make time at the end of the day to make a positive phone call home about a pupil, and be sure to use all forms of positive reinforcement as a means of formative assessment during PE lessons. Commonly, PE might be the only provider of positivity for a pupil. The rest of their school day could be particularly troublesome, and PE could be that shining light in their day that they look forward to and, in some cases, the only reason that they come into school at all. Within primary PE especially, reward through tangible means such as medals and certificates can be incredibly powerful. To this end, however, as previously discussed, keep track of your reward recipients and ensure a fair spread across classes throughout a term if possible.

Under this broad heading of 'Getting to Know Your Pupils' comes the importance of being able to learn, remember, and then recall names in lessons and within the wider school context. Now, former colleagues will be hurling accusations of hypocrisy in my direction, and they would be richly deserved. Being able to use names effectively is something that used to be a strength of my teaching, but most recently has slipped into my 'areas for development' section! Let's just put that down to old age!

One colleague within our department is quite simply incredible with his name recollection ability, and it is no coincidence that this quality helps him to develop positive working relationships with a wide range of his pupils. In addition, he is able to use his knowledge of pupil names to provide feedback succinctly and specifically to individuals, which automatically increases the powerful impact of formative assessment during the lesson. Furthermore, communication throughout a lesson is knitted together by using names when providing instruction in addition to feedback being provided. Challenging yourself to learn 5-10 new names per week can soon result in a vast knowledge of names that will begin to underpin your successful practice as a teacher.

An analogy that I often contemplate when considering lesson design and planning is that of a chef designing a restaurant menu. The chef would be branded naïve, and accused of borderline stupidity, if the restaurant continued to offer dishes to its patrons that nobody ever ordered, or that received consistently negative feedback. The same can be applied when considering elements to be included within a PE lesson. A practitioner that continually pedals a particular style, lesson activity, or medium-term plan that is not enjoyable or engaging for students is quite simply a practitioner that does not apply the required care or attention to their lesson delivery and planning. The most delicate aspect to consider in this instance is that it can be the case that the practitioner becomes oblivious or even dismissive to the perceptions of their pupils – this is when pupil voice becomes a vital tool to improve practice.

Pupil voice can be conducted formally or informally, and can take the form of a brief discussion or a formalised survey. Whether the aim is to extract qualitative or quantitative data, the most crucial aspects are to allow pupils to be honest, and for your samples to be inclusive of the groups in question. Avoid solely asking the pupil that lives and breathes sport whether they are enjoying PE lessons, as the feedback is likely to be positively skewed. By all means, include this pupil's feedback, but ensure that a cross-section of a group's views is considered.

It is also worth mentioning at this stage that this whole process might require an element of resilience from yourself as a practitioner. If you are anything like me, you'll not be that fond of receiving criticism and, having worked with many PE teachers, from my experience, the PE teacher is a very proud being! If feedback is critical, be sure to consider its context and validity, but do approach this entire process with an open mind, and a willingness to act upon the feedback provided. Making adaptations to delivery and practice on the back of pupil voice can be really empowering for pupils. Utilising pupils as co-designers of lessons can be incredibly powerful for pupils – 'Wow, we are actually being listened to, our voice matters!' – and for yourself as, hopefully, the outcome will result in more engaged and focused pupils.

Following effective usage of pupil voice, a clearer understanding of the 'sporting demographic' of a particular class should be achieved. The term 'sporting demographic' is one that I have coined during departmental meetings, and involves PE teachers proactively gaining an awareness of the sporting landscape in a class. It refers to members of teaching staff using several means, including pupil voice, to ascertain the activities, approaches and teaching styles that will result in the highest levels of engagement from all pupils. An approach I have encouraged with colleagues is for them to adapt and sometimes move away from curriculum design, in terms of activities to be covered, if the colleague provides a strong enough evidence base (pupil voice, student outcomes, engagement indicators) to suggest that the outcome will be higher engagement from all pupils.

Without entering too deeply into the 'depth vs breadth' debate with reference to PE curriculum, I strongly believe that there is no benefit at all in a teacher spending 6-8 weeks on an activity that goes completely against the 'sporting demographic' of a class. This isn't to suggest that the Y8 Boys group that love 'Foootttyyyyy' will get 39 weeks of football, but it could lead to football being a vehicle that could drive a dance block of work or could underpin delivery of health and fitness. Essentially, taking time to appreciate the context, history and sporting culture of a school and/or local area can lead to a greater understanding of the pupil population.

A further aspect of the profession that is made much more effective with preparation, and an understanding of pupils, is the Parents' Evening. There is no worse feeling than commencing a Parents' Evening appointment and being on the back foot from the off due to a lack of knowledge about the pupil being discussed. Parents can smell blood! They can sense the blagging and generic comments that are falling out of your mouth with no semblance of relevance, order, or meaning! I'll admit, I have suffered Parents' Evening appointments earlier in my career where I vowed never to put myself at such a high risk of dehydration as a result of excessive sweating and chronic dry mouth ever again!

In addition, with regards to Parents' Evenings, aim to be proactive in making appointments, or contacting home for those elusive pupils. Their elusiveness will usually be down to one of two reasons; the parents are unable to make or disinterested in making appointments, or the pupil has discouraged parents or carers from making an appointment for fear of reprimand from the home truths that could be delivered. In both instances, pupil contact can make a big difference, but requires a proactive approach to provide feedback that will ultimately be productive for that pupil.

As such, I always take an hour or so on the day to familiarise myself with the data linked to the class, and adopt a colour coding system that will allow a quick glance down as a prompt in the heat of battle, sorry, mid-appointment. I also try to make a note of activity-related specifics linked to each pupil. Even though I may not get the opportunity to glance down at these notes during the appointment, taking time to note them down during the day before allows this information to be fresh in my mind. Ultimately, however, the thread of this entire chapter applies to Parents Evenings', along with your day-to-day practice. If you adopt an approach of actively learning more about your pupils, their preferences and personalities, Parents' Evenings should be a relatively painless event. They should be able to serve their purpose of providing accurate and succinct feedback to parents, and in turn allow them to support their child to make ongoing and significant progress within physical education.

Top 3 Takeaways!

1. **Create class folders, with photos of your classes (following all things GDPR).**
   Next to each photo, make notes that will support delivery, but also help build and enhance relationships. What is this pupil interested in? What strategies work well to engage?

2. **Challenge yourself to learn 5 new pupil names a week.**
   Use names when meeting and greeting and throughout the school day.

3. **Make a positive phone call before you leave school at least 3 nights a week.**
   Share the positivity and recognise pupils that deserve to be recognised!

Chapter Reflection

Dr Colin Lewis, Senior Lecturer in physical education and sports coaching at Liverpool John Moores University. *@ColinLewis1989*

A fascinating read! As a Senior Lecturer in physical education in higher education, I consider the key points highlighted within the chapter to be of great benefit, and certainly thought-provoking. This chapter highlights the importance of building a caring relationship, to reflect upon how you currently communicate with your pupils, and finally how you can introduce strategies to develop an effective working relationship with your pupils. It undoubtedly makes you, as a practitioner, think whether you could do more to stimulate conversation with your pupils, and build caring relationships. This chapter offers plenty of learning opportunities for practitioners to take-home and consider, which, in turn, will hopefully enhance their understanding and knowledge of the importance of getting to know their pupils.

Specifically, drawing from the talking points within the chapter, these learning opportunities could include: (1) the significance of reinforcement and rewarding positive behaviours; (2) the need to empower the pupil voice, and why gathering feedback from a cross-section of a group is necessary to gather an honest and inclusive perspective of the groups in question; (3) to approach this entire process with an open mind and a willingness to act upon the feedback provided; and (4) how the use of first names, which has been explored and recommended previously in coaching behaviour research, is valuable when providing instruction, in addition to feedback, and as an effective way of developing positive working relationships. Indeed, the proposed challenge to learn 5-10 new names per week is by no means easy-going, but a challenge I would like to take on.

One additional thought that resonates with myself is the suggestion of communicating with pupils in reference to topics that might be considered to be 'outside' of the traditional classroom chatter (e.g.: did they watch the football at the weekend? Or asking pupils about their lives and interests, sporting or not). I concur that such a show of interest in the pupil as an individual is fitting in helping to develop mutual respect between the pupil and the practitioner and, in particular, to support behaviour management and/or engagement. This is certainly something that I will consider more, moving forwards, when presented with a challenging class.

To conclude, an investment of time and effort to engage and interact with pupils is central to supporting a pupil through their physical education experience. I am sure that the suggestions integrated within the chapter, and the takeaway messages proposed at the end of the chapter, will be absorbed by the readers, and will ultimately be empowering for young people, helping foster supporting and enjoyable sport and physical activity environments.

H

Home is for You!

Management of your work/life balance is a crucial and often overlooked aspect of being a successful PE teacher. Being able to separate school and home as places of work and leisure can support stress management and lead to a long, enjoyable, and successful PE teaching career!

I am sure that the vast majority of people that enter teaching are intending on a career that will span a great many years. For this to happen, a positive and healthy work/life balance is crucial. Being able to compartmentalise elements of your life will provide you with the required energy and stress management capability to consistently deliver in the workplace, whilst enjoying your craft. A happy teacher is an effective teacher.

As per 'Early Bird Gets the Worm', I like to give myself a head start regarding work-related tasks, by getting into school early in the morning. This habit, coupled with staying at work until my work-related tasks are complete, provides me with a balance and an approach where I take very little work home with me. This allows home to be a place where I can dedicate myself to my other jobs. Being a father, husband, and friend, as well as being able to focus on hobbies and activities that I like to be involved in too, which, not surprisingly, do involve sport!

I must stress, I have become slightly obsessive with this mantra to keep work at work and, yes, this can lead to my car being the last in the car park. However, I know that as soon as I pull away from school, my working day is done. This means tasks that teachers may traditionally take home such as lesson planning and marking (yes, don't believe the myth, PE teachers do have large amounts of marking too, which is made even more arduous when it is must be completed after an away fixture out of the county!), are completed at work, no matter how late a finish this may mean. This approach is the one that works for me. Yours may differ slightly. You may compartmentalise your day so that it is punctuated by other interests/hobbies – the gym, training, socialising, etc – but take time to find the routine/pattern that works for you and stick to it.

Furthermore, another useful message that I often repeat in my mind is that 'it will wait'. Now, you may feel that is a hypocritical perspective, but some tasks can wait until tomorrow, or even longer. It is about finding that balance between your work and your life. Managing your workload to preserve and cherish your positive mental health is essential. Imagine this hypothetical scenario: you have 8 mock GCSE PE examinations left to mark. It's 6pm. The deadline isn't until next Monday. Do you stay until they are finished or (in my case) do you leave them for another day so that you can get home to see the kids before bedtime? For you, it might be leaving them for another day so that you can go training, meet a friend, or quickly pop and see the parents. Yes, have that drive, that intrinsic motivation to work hard, but it must always be hand in hand with 'balance'.

Consistent communication is key, and hand in hand with this is the advice to conduct any required parental contact on the same day. From the parent's perspective, this provides them reassurance that any actions arising from a lesson are being dealt with swiftly and effectively by yourself as the teacher. It is also much more likely to have the desired impact, be it a communication with positive or negative ramifications, if it is done on the same day. Finally, staying that extra 5 (but sometimes much longer!) minutes to make that phone call can stop you taking any extra work-related worry home with you. The matter is dealt with, it is boxed off, and you can enjoy your evening without mulling the matter over and over in your mind. A teaching friend of mine used to finish each day with a positive phone call home. A great way to ensure that the working day concludes with a feel-good moment, in spite of how challenging the rest of the day has been.

An advantage of keeping work at work will be that you are able to dedicate time to your family and friends. From a family perspective, I appreciate that everyone reading this book will have a different situation, but the commonality for all is to try to maintain contact with family throughout your career. Your family will be incredibly proud of you and your achievements. Take time on a weekly basis to make contact and update them on your progress. Earlier in my career, due to the relentless cycle of teaching, assessment, fixtures, and the several other plates spinning in the air, I would go weeks without touching base with my mother, and this wasn't healthy for either of us. Build in time with loved ones into your schedules, even if this is at the sacrifice of your work as a PE Teacher. It is easy to lose sight of the most important aspects of your life but, trust me, your family will always be at the top of any list.

By the same virtue, make time for your friends, the friends you grew up with and those from outside of your work environment. I've seen many teachers become enveloped with their inner work circle of friends, often at the neglect of their friends from childhood, or external to the school context. Make time to engage with friends, enhance and cherish that support network. In addition, the last thing your friends out of school are going to want is to spend time with someone that is preoccupied with work emails pinging through on the phone out of hours. Most organisations are pretty hot with this at the moment and are keen to promote a healthy work/life balance. Remove the school email from the phone and dedicate your social time to being sociable!

Too often, teachers can narrow their friendship groups to just working colleagues. This can often lead to discussion focusing solely on work. People's disenchantment and negativity around work issues can become all-consuming. This is not healthy and can begin to impact performance as a teacher due to a lack of focus on classroom practice. This is, however, secondary to the negative impact it can have on your mental health. Now, this isn't to say that you should not have friends through work. Absolutely you should – some of my closest friends I have met through teaching, and I continue to consider my current colleagues as my closest friends. It is, however, once again, that term, 'balance'.

A further aspect to discuss within the remit of 'Home being for You' is your holidays. Undoubtedly, your non-teaching friends will level slanderous comments such as, 'You teachers get too many holidays' or, 'Are you ever at work?'. I personally love these comments, and always have an appropriate response prepared! Joking aside, however, the holidays are in their locations on the academic calendar and of their specific length because pupils, teachers, support staff, office staff, cleaners, catering staff, and all other auxiliary staff working within a school need that time to recharge, re-energise, relax, and maintain that 'balance' between their work and personal life.

This recharging of batteries during the holidays, in my experience, comes from integrating the advice from earlier in this chapter throughout the duration of the school holidays. Switch off from work, leave any work at school, it will wait. This might mean a bit of an extra push during the final week before a school holiday, taking the time to set up an enjoyable, work-free holiday period by working an extra hour to mark those coursework assignments, or by making those 3 or 4 positive phone calls home.

If it helps with the inevitable teaching guilt when you are enjoying yourself on a school holiday, remember two things:

1. The pupils need a break too; they will be fatigued and in need of a rest.
2. The vast majority of other teaching staff, certainly those with most experience, will not be even thinking about work, never mind using their holidays to do any work.

The same advice regarding the summer holidays applies to weekends too. Keeping your work and home lives separate can be crucial at weekends, especially midway through a long 7 or 8 week half term. That '5 on, 2 off' mentality can be crucial to keeping energy levels high, which, in turn, allows you time to be creative in your practice and provides you with the routine to reflect effectively.

My final aspect of advice linked to keeping the home a work-free haven is regarding most teachers' most hated communication tool…email! Many schools now adopt a policy and email strap-line that reads along the lines of, 'We believe in promoting a work-life balance and, as such, please do not expect a reply out of working hours. The realism of how many teachers and senior leaders actually adhere to this policy is alarmingly low! Try not to feel pressured into communicating via email on a night, weekend, or holiday. It can be tempting to reply in haste in order to mentally unload a request or response that has been sent in your direction via email but, equally, there can be no expectation from school leaders, colleagues, or parents for you to reply out of hours. Replying to an email during your free time can 'muddy the waters' of your mind, and lead to unnecessary thoughts regarding school and work. Leave the emails unread, remember, the 'Early Bird Gets the Worm', and respond during that extra 30-45 minutes you have bought yourself due to your incredible levels of punctuality!

There is a consistent thread running throughout this chapter, and being able to compartmentalise your working and social lives is crucial to maintaining your teaching longevity, and is inextricably linked to your performance levels as a practitioner. PE teachers that take time to consider their health and well-being are the most successful PE teachers within the profession. After all, we are huge advocates of health and well-being; it is important that after we talk the talk, we walk the walk!

Top 3 Takeaways!

1. **Make time within the next 10-14 days to meet with friends or family.**

2. **For the next week, try taking no work home at all.**
    Do not log on to your emails after hours, and disconnect from school when at home. Try this, see how it feels, and adopt it as your new routine if it feels like a positive change for the better!

3. **Plan your weekends ahead.**
    You plan your working week, be sure to plan your weekend to maximise them to their fullest potential, even if this just to relax, planning blank weekends is great too!

Chapter Reflection

Warren Dutton, Director of Education LLS and the Steven Gerrard Academy, Former PE and English Teacher, Head of PE, Director of Sport and Assistant Headteacher
@LLSonline

A good work life balance is very easy to talk about and often difficult to implement. The best teachers are highly dedicated, committed to all aspects of the job, and determined to give their best at all times. Approximately 1/3 of all staff who enter the profession leave within five years, with workload often cited as a reason for leaving.

We, as a profession, must find ways to become highly effective without burning out, or experiencing detrimental effects on our relationships and mental and physical well-being. Ben has made a number of purposeful suggestions as to what works for him in this chapter, which relates to work being in work and home being at home. I think dedicating time to tasks is essential in trying to strike a work-life balance, whether that is in the school building or at home. I use calendar invites to put artificial time limits on tasks, which has reduced procrastination and meant that non-contact time is used much more efficiently. The calendar can also be used to put in things like 'walking lunch', 'personal reading', '10-minute catch ups', and 'meetings' into your working week, so there are things to look forward to, allowing you to work on personal well-being. We wouldn't miss a meeting with a parent or a HOD, so we need to make these 'meetings' equally important.

Ben's words on 'what can wait' are also important, being able to close work in a place you are comfortable with. It's sometimes useful to come up with your own system to deal with 'to do lists', which might include today, this week, and this month, as examples. Quiet time, at the beginning of the day, is the perfect time to deal with tasks that require deeper cognitive thinking before the bedlam that is a school day begins. Non-contact time is often over before it has begun, by the time a changing room has been cleared, equipment has been collected or set up, you have returned from the far reaches of school, or the million and one other jobs including fixtures, kit, transport, and phone calls. I would actively encourage senior staff and HOD's to consider how non-contact is distributed. Can non-contact be put together so staff have two sessions, for example, and does that have to be spent on site? It may be really helpful for staff to see families, or simply to go to a gym, do yoga, or play golf.

Overwhelmingly, it's about trying to compartmentalise your time, and not allowing commitment to school to become overbearing, and eventually untenable. An important chapter to make us stop and think about our own schedule and routines.

I

Inclusivity is Key!

Adopting a mindset of inclusivity throughout your working practices as a PE teacher can lead to higher pupil engagement and participation in physical activity.

Inclusivity within physical education is vital when looking to create lifelong, active habits for all pupils. I often view inclusivity as the removal of barriers to participation. These barriers are often wide-ranging and unique. As a practitioner, if you adopt a routine of foreseeing how an aspect of a lesson or departmental procedure might be perceived by a pupil, this is always a good starting point to preventing exclusivity, and encouraging an inclusive, positive learning environment for all.

The process of anticipating pupil perception of a lesson or activity is a form of mental imagery coupled with empathy. Try to anticipate the feelings, emotions, activity levels, and level of challenge that will exist within a lesson. It is also important to try and perceive a lesson from the viewpoints of several pupils from the class. This is not just about how much the county cricketer will enjoy the lesson you have planned on the intricacies of swing bowling as, yes, the county cricketer's perception will most likely be very positive, but how about the other 29 pupils in the class? This would be an example of a lesson being planned without the needs of the whole class in mind. In this instance, a smarter approach would be for the cricket bowling lesson to be limitless in its design. Allow all pupils to work on their bowling with conditions applied that will provide a positive learning environment for all abilities, then adapt the activity by increasing or decreasing the level of challenge or complexity. If the activity levels are kept high (often through ensuring that pupils have access to performing the skill at quick and regular intervals, with queueing for a turn removed through activity design), then the opportunity could arise for you to spend some time with the county cricketer to look at the grip of the ball, seam position etc. Alternatively, you could look to utilise the high levels of subject knowledge from the cricketer in the class and assign them with a coaching brief to work with the other pupils. In addition, ensure time is spent with the disengaged and less focused. I have often observed teachers spend more time with the high end than those that are struggling, perhaps as a form of affirmation for the content and delivery being received by the few to vindicate the purpose of the lesson, as opposed to acknowledging less engaged pupils. Your time and energy should always focus on all, not just a few.

By definition, it could be termed that an inclusive PE lesson is one that has all pupils engaged, challenged, learning, and active throughout. As such, lesson design should focus on maximising activity whilst minimising inactivity. Avoid activities that can exclude a pupil, activities where a pupil is considered 'out'. Obviously, this doesn't spell the end for activities such as cricket, rounders and softball, but considerations around the conditions to be applied should always be to maximise activity time. Aim to avoid scenarios that lead to a pupil being left out when they are out. Quick rotations of roles, losing runs instead of exclusion, and modifying the activity to even avoid a pupil being 'out' are all ways to enhance the inclusivity of a lesson.

Sports that include a pupil being 'out' are the most obvious when focusing on exclusivity, but most classical invasion activities are at risk of seeing pupils being excluded from activity time if the lesson design is complacent or neglectful. To focus on two examples in particular, football and netball, the traditional curriculum staple activity areas, both these activities can be prone to exclusivity if the practitioner fails to address the potential lesson experiences of all pupils.

With football, I am hard pushed to find a situation during a lesson, even moving towards GCSE or A Level study, where a practitioner could strongly argue a case for a full sided 11 v 11 match to be taking place. The first potential issue is ensuring that the ability levels of both teams are equal. Any inequality between the teams will lead to many students being excluded by the nature of the gameplay that is to follow. Another issue revolves around all of the action being in one area of the pitch, dominated by 2-3 stronger pupils, meaning that an entire goalkeeper and defence from one team would be redundant, along with the forward line of the other. Do not feel pressured by the cries of, 'Sir, Miss, when are we having a match' to feel that this means a full sided game. Differentiated 3 v 3 ladder tournaments that include the conditions or theme of the lesson are much more inclusive, and will allow pupils to demonstrate their levels whilst maximising activity time.

Even concepts such as positional responsibilities, and defending and attacking as a team, can be covered through small-sided, conditioned games. Within football too, and this is perhaps the most obvious element of advice I will write, please ensure a rotation system is in place for any lesson scenario that involves a goalkeeper. Trust me, as obvious as this may be to you, I have witnessed vastly experienced teachers allow one pupil to spend an entire lesson in goal, in November, in the rain, just off the coast of the North Sea!

Much of the above can also apply to netball. At this stage, I am fearing the wrath of many PE teachers (and my wife as a netball player and coach!) as I mildly chastise netball, but I'm afraid that I have too often witnessed such lacklustre delivery of the sport: delivery that includes extended periods of gameplay wherein a Goal Shooter and Opposing Goalkeeper have the opportunity to have a good catch up whilst fending off the mild effects of hyperthermia, as all the gameplay is in the other circle, where 13 girls watch one poor goal shooter take 10 attempts to score into a net that is at full adult height and nigh on impossible for the year 7 to reach! With netball, consider rotation of positions or roles within lessons, consider smaller sided activities, 3 v 2's, 3 v 3's, consider adaptation of rules to assist with activity in the lessons, be creative in your design to allow pupils to achieve lesson outcomes that hopefully focus on activity, engagement, and progress. Many NGBs provide resources and guidance on how to modify activity to promote inclusivity – be sure to research and experiment when possible.

Inclusivity, and all the considerations recommended above, becomes even more vital for our pupils in Key Stages 1 and 2. During a pupil's formative years, lifelong perceptions of physical activity and PE can be formed. Positive experiences will lead to the 'hook', the 'buzz', the excitement and the anticipation that builds when it is PE day. Exclusive, negative PE experiences can lead to reticence, disinterest, and reluctance to engage with physical education at all.

This theme of inclusivity throughout physical education extends to extra-curricular programmes. This is often achieved by the concepts and approaches applied by PE teachers. In a later chapter, this book will explore the importance and value of extra-curricular opportunities, but with reference specifically to inclusivity; PE teachers must work hard to create a culture and environment that will encourage pupils to commit their time to extra participation in physical activity. Avoid language or processes that could make a pupil feel they are not welcome, or worthy of attending an extracurricular club. I class the first participation of an anxious or traditionally 'non-sporty' pupil at an extracurricular club as a fantastic achievement for our department. The only way this achievement is bettered is when that pupil goes from attending once, to attending twice, to attending regularly, until it becomes habitual for them to come along. This illustrates that, as a department, we are doing the right things in lessons to engage young people in physical activity. Ensure the extracurricular offer is accessible to all, and is void of any barriers such as ability levels or overly-elitist climates, and wide-ranging participation levels will remain consistently high.

As mentioned earlier, inclusivity within PE is essentially the removal of barriers that could prevent high levels of participation in lessons, and participation in extracurricular opportunities. This concept can be at its most challenging when working with pupils with SEND (Special Educational Needs and Disabilities). Try not to become too daunted when that moment arises when you receive a class list and realise that you are to teach a pupil with SEND; equally, remove any preconceptions you may have, ensuring you approach with positivity and open-minded nature. There is a multitude of research and literature that has been produced and, whilst I shall not enter into specific SEND conditions throughout this book, my first area of advice is to take the time to do background reading on the area of SEND diagnosis of a pupil you are due to teach.

Secondly, I would always recommend that a teacher takes time to contact the parent/carer of the pupil. Take time to discuss the barriers (or absence of barriers – I have often had an ill-judged preconception that a pupil may have a negative attitude towards physical education, and these are dispelled by a parent/carer) and, ultimately, the parent/carer will be able to discuss the unique and bespoke methods that work effectively with their child. Taking these methods and consistency into your lessons will only make for a more positive experience for SEND pupils within physical education.

Be sure once again to access the available support within schools. Speak to colleagues with experience, and share experiences of working with SEND in the past. Also, make time to meet with the school SENDCO/SENCO (Special Educational Needs and Disability Coordinator) and, if available, request a lesson observation from them, and take on board all feedback and advice; all of these steps and procedures are examples of proactivity that will make you feel more prepared prior to delivery.

Finally, be sure to guide and utilise any teaching assistants or support available to you during lessons. Taking the time to explain their role during a lesson and the rationale behind your decision can empower a member of support staff to provide you with the assistance to make the lesson a positive and inclusive learning experience for all pupils. Often, the teaching assistant will have a much greater experience of working with SEND and a particular pupil, tapping into their knowledge can be invaluable. Also, be sure to have interaction with the pupils. Whilst further developing that positive teacher/pupil relationship, you can dig deep as to the pupil's feelings towards PE: do they feel challenged and supported to make progress? Working with pupils in this way can empower and inspire, with the pupil feeling that their voice is being heard.

Essentially, in lessons and during extracurricular time, think all, not some. Be welcoming, not exclusive. Be considerate of all the young people that you work with, and make physical education accessible to all by skilfully removing the barriers that are personal and individualised to each pupil within a school.

Top 3 Takeaways!

1. **When planning your next lesson, prioritise an increased focus on inclusivity in activity design.**
   Think how you can ensure all pupils are equally active, challenged and engaged.

2. **When teaching alongside teaching assistants, be sure to communicate the role of the TA prior to the lesson.**
   Be clear how they can support SEND pupils in lessons.

3. **Review your extracurricular commitment.**
   Is there a club or activity you can offer that will engage the traditionally challenging to engage? Propose this to your head of department.

Chapter Reflection

Ryan Forwood, Primary PE Lead and AfPE Leadership and Influence Award Winner 2021. @RyanForwoodPE

As a practitioner, I acknowledge the importance of inclusivity within every single lesson I teach. I remember taking part in a rugby session where I was being coached; it was raining and freezing on a winter evening. We were standing still for extended periods of time. The rest of the team and I were shivering, and felt ourselves switching off, whilst the coach was nice and warm in his massive jacket, clearly not considering how we were feeling in the moment. As explained in this chapter, empathy is key. Reading about the student who was asked to 'spend an entire lesson in goal, in November, in the rain, just off the coast of the North Sea!' brought me back to how I felt myself in my scenario of being coached in rugby. Being fresh into my teaching career, I remember thinking at the time that I would always consider what each and every student felt like during my lessons. 'The process of anticipating pupil perception of a lesson or activity is a form of mental imagery coupled with empathy', is something that every educator should make that link to from their experiences, which puts their enjoyment of physical activity in jeopardy.

This chapter highlights the essential aspect of the 'affective' domain, and places creating a 'positive learning environment' at the heart of planning. I once had a conversation with @ IMSporticus on Twitter, who stated that the role of our job can be explained as 'not putting them off' when it comes to being active. Students can be turned off from physical activity easily and, on the other hand, if they have positive environments to learn in, the likelihood of said students seeking opportunities beyond the curriculum increases. As this chapter also discusses, this could include extracurricular activities within the school. Increased numbers of students coming back week after week must have a greater significance over creating a smaller percentage of elite performers.

The chapter highlights the importance of differentiation and pedagogy. As a primary PE lead, the curriculum content stating 'modified where appropriate' when approaching playing competitive games is vital when it comes to inclusivity. 3v3 over 11v11 in traditional games will have a massive impact on ensuring all students feel valued and included. This can enable students of all abilities, experiences and SEND diagnoses, to achieve their potential.

This chapter provides essential points for practitioners to consider when it comes to ensuring the highest standards of physical education, physical activity, and school sport in their settings.

J

Join In!

Fully submerging yourself into the school or context you are working within will ultimately underpin your success. No half measures, get stuck in, embrace the culture and ethos of the school and department, and be that asset to the team that you know you can be!

Being willing to embrace the ethos of a PE department, and able to appreciate how physical education fits into the overall machine of a particular school, can be crucial when considering your success, during either a placement or full-time employment.

Physical education as an entity, a subject, and a priority will sit differently within every school across the world. This may be because of a national directive, government legislation, pressures from governing bodies, stronger agendas directed from OFSTED and, commonly, the perceptions of the departmental SLT link or the senior leadership team as a whole. There is a likelihood here that those higher up the hierarchy will have a strong PE influence – such is the regularity with which PE specialists are successful in middle and senior leadership positions in schools. As such, it is important that you ascertain and understand the position of physical education and its priorities within a school quickly. This will enable you to play your role within the greater team and help the department work towards their collective aim.

This isn't always an easy task, to be able to intuit the culture and ethos of physical education within a school. It isn't something that is always written down, advertised, or tangible to pupils and staff. This is where you must be proactive in getting that sense and feel for physical education within a school. During observation periods, be sure to note down any commonalities in delivery across a department. Do they adopt consistent policies regarding kit, sharing of objectives, or through lesson design? In addition, request time with departmental leads to talk to them about their vision for physical education. All of the departmental leads I have worked with and met at other schools are passionate in sharing their views and opinions relating to PE. Absorb them, and consider how you can become an effective member of the team. This advice is applicable to all career stages, and well worth revisiting as you move through your career. Taking stock, and reflecting whether the vision or ethos for PE has changed, is also a worthwhile practice.

This notion of being a team member is, for me, multi-layered. It is much more than just toeing the party line. Take the metaphorical analogy that you see on TV shows when a team of people are carrying a log up a hill; if one team member stops or slows down, the rest of the team are required to take on or absorb their workload. The same applies within a PE department. If a departmental policy is in place, its application is your responsibility. Take the age-old battle of pupils wearing jewellery or incorrect (usually just their black school socks) kit for PE. If the rest of the department are clamping down on these issues and you are not, this not only undermines colleagues, it negatively tarnishes your reputation as being the 'lenient one' but, most importantly, goes against departmental and school-wide drives around standards.

When considering the wider school machine, it is vital that you remember that not only is PE an important cog in the functionality of a school but you too, from a personal perspective, are equally as vital. Too often, the microcosmic nature of PE departments can lead to isolation, dissonance with the whole school approach, and an 'Us and Them' mentality. This can be damaging to the wider school movement towards shared goals, but also your personal development and progression.

PE can often approach a whole school focus from a different angle than most other subject areas. Take literacy/reading for example. I know from my own personal experiences as an adolescent and adult that much of my reading was sport-related. Positive modelling from a PE department can be incredibly powerful towards a wider school drive on reading and literacy. To this end, the growth of World Book Day fancy dress has been remarkable and, in the past, I have been guilty of mocking the whole concept. My attitudes had to, and have, changed. The tenuous dressing up as a sporting icon from yesteryear proved very powerful. It sparked conversations about reading habits and sport and further worked to develop positive relationships with pupils. Also from my experience, being proactive on whole school initiatives can be very beneficial when applying for an internal promotion, as leaders are rightly keen to know that you are a team player, especially when moving towards middle or senior leadership positions.

Within a PE environment, be forthcoming and 'Join In' by helping colleagues. PE is a unique entity when it comes to the adaptability required by staff, especially when considering the impact of fixtures, weather, exams in sports halls, staff absence, and the several members of the department that will undoubtedly have additional areas of responsibility within the school.

The 'Double Up' lessons will happen – they are inevitable – and it is all about rolling up your sleeves and getting the job done. Ultimately, you will require a colleague to do the exact same for you on many occasions during your career. Equally, the covering of extracurricular clubs or fixtures will also be requests received at your door. Once again, you will probably require this from a colleague in the future. It is about knuckling down for the greater good and being a valuable member of the team.

Moving the focus to joining in within lessons, there comes the often-contentious issue of teacher demonstrations. Personally, I would encourage you to be brave enough to try and always demonstrate the skills and techniques that you are aiming to deliver within practical lessons. Demonstrating a skill provides a visual base for learners to attempt to replicate themselves. When demonstrating, consider the visual being provided to all learners in a class by providing different angles and viewpoints if possible. I often find 'slo-mo' demonstrations accompanied with succinct, accurate teaching points are particularly useful. In addition, a continued demonstration whilst a full group attempts a technique can provide an ongoing visual to support short-term memory.

There will be a number of skills and techniques that you might consider areas of weakness, but be brave, work on these areas like you expect your pupils to work on them in lessons. Practise and refine them; this will improve the quality of your technique, and also provide an insight into the experience of your pupils. How did you feel when you attempted to conquer a challenging skill area? This empathy for your pupils should support your delivery and patience when working with classes. This said, you are allowed to share your own vulnerabilities with pupils. Do not become burdened with an unrealistic expectation that you must be a master of all skill areas from a curriculum. As my colleagues will testify, I am possibly the worst trampolinist in western Europe. My demonstrations stretch to a 5 bounce sequence on the cross. For everyone's benefit, I do not attempt any skills of remote difficulty; pupils are aware of this vulnerability in my armour, and I believe it just demonstrates that I am a human being, with strengths and weaknesses, just like them.

As a pupil myself, I did very little athletics due to the lack of facilities at my inner-city school. As a result, during my placement at a strong athletics school, I had to address my subject knowledge weaknesses. I also wanted to have that aforementioned empathy and appreciation for the learning processes that would be experienced by my pupils. I used my non-contact periods as an opportunity to go out onto the field with a javelin – YouTube tutorial on my phone – and make 100s of throws until I felt confident with the discipline. Too often, PE teachers adopt an 'I can't do that' mentality to certain sports, where I believe they owe it to their pupils to at least 'have a go', at even the most basic levels of demonstration. Pupils will often appreciate your efforts, and it can have a positive impact on pupil-teacher relationships.

This said, for more advanced skills and techniques, you will often be blessed with an in-class expert in the shape of a pupil with out-of-school experience in the activity area being covered. Utilising these pupils can be a huge confidence boost to the demonstrating pupil, and the rest of the class, as it could be used to create an 'if they can do it, so can I' mentality amongst pupils.

The common theme throughout this chapter is to be committed to your school, department, and subject. Step out of the comfort zone, and you will be rewarded with growth and development that will support your progression as a PE teacher.

Top 3 Takeaways!

1. **During non-contact time, conduct a department-wide observation.**
    Have a walk through several lessons in an hour (lesson length) and make note of commonalities in practice.

2. **Ahead of your next lesson out of specialism, factor in time prior to delivery to practise skill elements that could require demonstration.**

3. **Be sure to participate in whole school, non-PE projects.**
    Get out of the PE office, and use your role positively in a new area.

Chapter Reflection

Rebecca Bridges, Head of Physical Education based in Lancashire, England.
@Becky_Bridges

Initially, when reading the title of this chapter, I believed it must surely be about how, as passionate sports people, we are tempted to 'join in' with the teaching PE (which I am guilty of – I will challenge anybody to a basketball shootout!). But this chapter was so much more than that.

This chapter reflects on how PE fits into the wider machine of the school, and how PE can be a catalyst towards developing a whole school-ethos and culture, as well as personal career progression.

There is some advice throughout this chapter that certainly resonated with me, especially around capturing department commonalities, such as kit, and the sharing of objectives. It is vitally important when seeking out a career as a PE teacher to see whether you would 'gel' with that department, and reflect on whether your vision, views, and opinions align with those of the department/school. If you feel as though something isn't quite right, or you don't feel that the department's vision and values align with your own, don't be too afraid to say it's not the right place for you.

This chapter also reflects on being a team player within a department, notably when applying department-wide policy, such as that on jewellery and kit, and uses the analogy of a team of people carrying a log up a hill. This could not be truer of the realities of working in a successful PE department. You have to work as a team and, when I reflect on the numerous PE departments I have worked in, those that are the most successful are not always those that have the best of friends, who socialise regularly together, but those who have each other's backs, respect one another professionally, and listen to each other respectfully.

Being a PE teacher can be tough at times, and the uncertain nature of various things that could happen throughout the school day, such as poor weather, staff absence, fixtures, and exams in the sports hall are all discussed throughout this chapter. When I reflected on this, I realised that I am a firm believer that we can only control the controllables in life. I recently listened Jonas Salzgeber's on the 'Believe, Move, Grow' Podcast who referred to the Reserve Clause and the Process. Jonas spoke of the 'Stoic Archer' where one imagines you have a bow and arrow, and the goal is to hit the target. If you focus only on the things you control, i.e.: the bow you choose or the training you put into the action (focusing on the process), then the moment you release the arrow the outcome is not within your control. If the arrow is blown off course by a gust of wind, this doesn't matter to the Stoic Archer, as they try their best and accept the outcome with equanimity. The Reserve Clause prepares oneself to accept the outcome with equanimity, i.e.: I will try my best, but I am aware I may not succeed, as something outside of my control may interfere. This will prepare a person if things don't go as planned. I thought this philosophical thinking could be applied in multiple contexts for people within education, sport and life, and is a nod to focusing on the process, not obsessing about the outcome.

Throughout this chapter, I found myself nodding along, especially when the chapter discusses whining. Plenty of times, I have been the teacher this chapter advises us not to be, those 'double up' lessons do happen – someone might have taken the equipment you need, or taken the pupil you really needed in that revision lesson out,. As discussed earlier, a multitude of things can happen in a school day to throw you off guard from the perfect planning that you may have done, but, as this chapter says, 'No one wants to hear you whining'.

Addressing subject knowledge is poignant throughout this chapter, and is great advice for any PE teacher starting out. Even now, 7 years in, I am still always learning, and every year I change the way I teach each activity based on what I see my own department do, and what I may discover on Twitter/YouTube. It's certainly easy to become 'stagnant', and continue to teach shot put, for example, in the same way you have always taught shot put. The advice to spend free periods watching others is invaluable, and something I am always advising my own department to do, and something which I know they have valued.

In summary, this chapter promotes honest reflection, and emphasises the need for constant learning and adaptation in practice. As the chapter finishes, step out of your comfort zone, and you will indeed be rewarded with growth and development that will support your progression as a PE teacher.

K

Know Your Craft!

The ever-changing world of physical education and teaching leads to a higher than ever devotion to the profession and your craft. Keeping up to date with developments linked to the curriculum and your delivery is crucial, and will ultimately keep your practices current and relevant.

The art of the 'blag'. You will all know someone in your life that is a 'blagger', and the chances are that your levels of respect for this person are pretty low. This also transfers to PE teaching. You may have delivered a coaching session or PE lesson, walked away and thought, 'I just completely blagged my way through that'. I am going to guess at this point that, if this is the case, you probably didn't enjoy the experience, and felt high levels of anxiety throughout. The anxiety was so unbearable due to a fear of being 'caught out'.

Now, if you haven't fully been in a position where you have been caught out, chances are you might have been in a position where a pupil puts you on the spot with a sport-specific question to which you did not have the answer. This happens to every PE teacher on the planet, I hasten to add. The main difference being that the strongest PE teachers will make sure that it isn't an overly-repeated experience, by going away and addressing any subject knowledge gaps that a pupil has exposed, much to the teacher's horror and discomfort!

The common physical education curriculum during an academic year will cover between 10 and 15 different sporting activities. As such, to be expected to be an expert or master in all of these activities is completely unrealistic. It is not unrealistic, however, for you to take the time to become familiar with the key rules, terminologies and basic technical aspects of an activity that you are expected to teach with clarity to your pupils. Now, how you go about this is completely down to you and how you learn best. Options include YouTube tutorials, collaboration with experienced colleagues, conducting reading from coaching manuals linked to the activity, or enrolling yourself onto relevant coaching courses.

Opinion can be split regarding a PE trainee enrolling on to several coaching courses prior to commencing their training. Many feel that coaching courses can be too driven towards future coaches of that particular sport and that, often, the context of the course delivery lacks relevance to a school/physical education setting. This criticism has been addressed by many governing bodies who offer more professional development style courses for teachers, providing advice and ideas that PE teachers can apply to their lessons.

Hopefully, guidance will arrive in the form of your ITT (university tutor) or school mentor, who will be able to recommend courses based upon your experience, confidence, and requirements of the current curriculum. This was certainly the case when I began my training. My mentor made it a condition that I enrolled onto level 1 courses in volleyball and hockey. These activities highlighted themselves as areas of development through my letter of application and interview for my PGCE. I can only speak from personal experience, but I am extremely grateful that I took the time to undertake a level 1 in both these areas, as it provided me with the basic levels of subject knowledge to begin my PE teaching journey, and had led to them (through years of delivery and critical reflection) being activities that I now enjoy delivering, something I would not have believed at the start of my career.

In the absence of guidance from a mentor, be proactive. I have mentioned the word 'audit' in previous chapters. With regards to subject knowledge, work your way through the areas of the National Curriculum, and give yourself a score out of ten. For your lowest scoring 3-4 areas, make a note of the exact aspect that is causing you concern within that activity. Is it practical ideas? Rules? Terminology? Then plan on how you will address this. Remember, there is no activity out of bounds to a PE teacher within a curriculum. As a Head of PE, one of my biggest annoyances is when I hear PE teachers say, 'I don't deliver _____'. This is wholly unacceptable. Does a maths teacher just swerve the algebra section? No. They upskill, practice, and ready themselves for classroom delivery – this premise is exactly the same within physical education. If, at this moment, you feel you are not ready to deliver a curriculum area, make sure you take the appropriate steps to be ready for that first lesson, which might be much sooner than you think.

Taking the opportunity to move away from practical aspects of physical education for a moment, there is also the likelihood that you will have some involvement in, if not total responsibility for, the delivery of examination courses during your placement and/

or first contract of employment. This can often be a daunting prospect, mainly due to the perceived increase in accountability that you have for pupil outcomes. My advice here is, once again, to ensure that you have done your due diligence regarding the examination course being delivered at your centre. In addition, and this may sound obvious, ensure you are up to date with developments from the examination awarding body. These can be frequent, and you owe it to the pupils to ensure that you are completely up to speed with any changes in content, weightings, or examination design. Regularly visiting examination board websites and enrolling yourself on the appropriate continual professional development (CPD) that is offered for examination PE is strongly recommended. Maintain communication with teachers from other centres that are also responsible for delivery of examination physical education. If you are unsure, ask. The answers will be out there, but only if you are proactive in going out to find them.

An earlier chapter touched upon a valuable element of advice when considering the delivery of examination or theory-based lessons. Developing a resource bank of materials is vital, and utilising the brilliant network of physical educators can support you from the perspective of broadening your teaching horizons; they can provide an alternative approach to delivering theory content, but help save you time, which is crucial in preventing burn-out and fatigue in PE teachers. If you are borrowing resources from another source, please take the time to tailor them to your pupils' needs. Consistency in the design and branding of PowerPoints, for example, can support the learning of pupils. Essentially, the advice here is, by all means use resources developed by someone else, but take time prior to delivery to make them consistent with your delivery and your school and/or department. From my own personal experience, pupils are very quick to recognise the lack of personal planning that has gone into a lesson; this is not an enjoyable experience at all.

When considering knowledge in physical education, try not to become complacent. Avoid becoming a 'know it all' because it is your area of relative expertise, and please avoid being a practitioner that delivers lessons in a certain style, using the same activities, and follows it up with the phrase, 'this is how I have always done it'. This phrase is dangerous,as it can breed complacency and lead to practitioners becoming stagnant in their teaching. Aim to explore, experiment, and even reinvent your teaching. For areas of the curriculum that you are able to just about 'scrape by', be proactive and address this. Strengthen and deepen your knowledge of activities and broader pedagogy by investing time and energy into the research or practice method that best suits you and, more importantly, your pupils. Teachers learn in very different and unique ways. Some will learn by reading, others by watching video clips, others by experimenting out on the field or in the sports hall. Tailor your learning to best suit you, but challenge yourself to continuously learn – have that inner drive to not accept mediocrity in your teaching.

Ultimately, there will not be a moment in your career where you will have learned everything, or absorbed every aspect of knowledge linked to PE teaching. During my 13 years in the profession, there have been changes in government, changes in staffing, and changes in sporting rules and guidelines that have all led to an importance in ensuring that my subject knowledge levels across the curriculum are maintained to the highest possible levels.

For those at the earliest stages of the PE teaching journey, avoid being a narrow practitioner that has their few areas of expertise, and will manipulate lessons and opportunities to only work within these areas. You will be a much more valuable asset and attractive proposition to a PE department with a continuous and proactive approach to your learning. This isn't a full-time coaching role within a single sport. This is a teaching position that I believe requires more versatility than any other subject in a school. Ensure that you are equally versatile, and you will become an invaluable member of any PE department.

Top 3 Takeaways!

1. **Sign up for non-PE, teacher-based CPD, online or in school, that will support your development.**

2. **Set aside time to research a curriculum activity area in more depth.**
   Consider its history, rules, strategies, and any other aspects that can broaden your knowledge.

3. **Use your immediate network.**
   Speak to colleagues and peers regarding areas of subject knowledge development and request support.

Chapter Reflection

Kirtsty Bundy, University of Lincoln, Senior Lecturer in PE & Sport. *@BundyKirsty*

In my opinion, there are three important messages in 'Know your Craft', centred around the importance of continual professional development (CPD) for PE teachers, and the various means by which this can be accessed.

First, for those developing their careers in schools, they can, of course, access CPD through in-house programs, but these will typically involve generic developmental courses, mainly related to the whole school development plan and the current developments in education. However, for more case-specific, bespoke CPD, PE teachers should also determine their own performance management targets, and use a wide range of easily accessible platforms to support specific development needs. There are some wonderful, socially recognised practitioners out there who are very happy to share their ideas! It is up to PE teachers to explore the wide range of resources available outside of whole school CPD, National Governing Body courses, and subject-specific teacher awards.

Second, the chapter emphasises the importance of building your own resource bank. This is perhaps one of the most valuable messages, and I have certainly tried it throughout my career. Every day is a new challenge, and you should consider your career as a working document. You should review the resources you are using regularly, or at least every time you have used them, update them, and discuss them with colleagues. You should not be afraid to try something new, or something which may not work – you may even surprise yourself!

Third, a very important message is given in the chapter around utilising a range of teaching styles within lessons. Moston and Ashworth (1994) identify two clear types of teaching styles: productive and reproductive. Some activities naturally lean towards the reproductive style of teaching, such as those with technical and health and safety considerations, where the teacher being in control is deemed important. Productive styles are favoured within those activities where the element of risk is lower, and children are free to lead their own learning (Chatoupis, 2018) Usually, one style doesn't always fit all circumstances, but a successful PE teacher will use one or several styles within their lessons, trying to find the combination that best meets learners' needs, and at the same time start creating a 'toolbox' of strategies (Sanchez et al., 2011) and resources that can be reused in the future. To sum up, the message I get from the chapter is around getting the basics right and developing your own philosophy, while continuing to develop your subject knowledge and pedagogical skills and accumulating a range of resources; then you can afford to experiment and refine your craft to become the continually evolving teacher who meets the needs of all children (Burton, 2018).

References

- Burton, D. (2018) *Teach Now! Physical education. Becoming a great PE teacher.* Routledge. London
- Chatoupis, C. C. (2018) 'Physical education Teachers' Use of Mosston and Ashworth's Teaching Styles: A Literature Review', *The Physical Educator*, 75, pp. 880-900. https://doi.org/10.18666/TPE-2018-V75-I5-8292
- Sanchez, B., Byra, M. & Wallhead, T.L. (2012) 'Students' perceptions of the command, practice, and inclusion styles of teaching', *Physical education and Sport Pedagogy*, 17:3, pp. 317-330, DOI: 10.1080/17408989.2012.690864
- White, P. T. (1998). Perceptions of physical education majors and faculty members regarding the extent of use of and exposure to Mosston's: Mosston and Ashworth's spectrum of teaching styles Dissertation Abstracts International, 59 (5), p. 1508A University Microfilms No. AAG9834533

L

Learn to Blow a Whistle

Developing a presence within a range of teaching environments enables a PE teacher to share instructions succinctly, minimise low-level disruption, and create a positive learning environment that supports the development of a range of learners.

It is very clear why most non-PE specialists despise being given a cover lesson of PE. The classic range of PE teaching environments takes a non-PE specialist way out of their comfort bubble of the classroom. The noise, space, movement, and organisational skills required to effectively utilise sporting equipment are all completely alien to non-PE teachers. The non-PE specialist (this section is not simply to berate classroom teachers, I hasten to add) has the consistency of the classroom, displays, whiteboard, seating plans, and many more variables under their control. In contrast, the PE teacher must adapt from a sports hall to a field, from a dance studio to a swimming pool, and from a fitness suite to a theory lesson in a classroom. On occasions, that all happens within a day's teaching. The acoustics of these facilities all differ greatly, and an effective practitioner must subtly modify delivery and communication styles in order to suit the teaching environments mentioned above. And all of that before we even consider the logistics around changing rooms and movement to teaching spaces.

The title of this chapter is inspired by the numerous trainees I have observed that, usually early on in a placement, lack presence within a PE teaching environment. This is often illustrated by the trainee being unable to blow a whistle with any modicum of authority. The air exhaled would barely cause the pea to rattle around the interior of the whistle, and the noise emanating from it would barely rouse the attention of a dormouse, never mind 30 excitable year 9 boys. In my experience, for all these trainees, there has been a correlation between the quality of their whistle blowing and the level of presence they assert in a lesson. You may, however, have noticed that I mentioned that this is usually early on during a teaching placement? This is because, as with all elements of teaching, it is an aspect that can be addressed through observation and effective reflection.

Now, commonly, people will throw a mythical opinion that 'some people were born to teach' or that 'they will quite simply never be able to hold a presence within a lesson'. These are wholly inaccurate. Development of a presence as a PE teacher may happen at different speeds for different practitioners, but I am a firm believer that it can be developed in everyone. At this juncture, please do not mistake presence for volume. Yes, a teacher with presence will be able to apply the appropriate levels of volume to their voice and their whistle to control, progress, organise, and challenge a PE class, but the notion of presence is much more multi-layered than a good old shout or rollicking of a disobedient class. We will have all been in a situation, either during our schooling or whilst playing for a sports team, where you will have had to sit through an old-fashioned rollicking. My personal response in this situation was to completely switch off; I had a knack of being able to make my face look as though I was listening, but the reality was that I was happily daydreaming about something completely different. In addition, these rants were commonly not even directed towards me. I was having to experience the rollicking by the simple virtue of being present in the classroom or changing room, while this teacher or coach was taking his or her frustrations from another aspect of their life out on us. This style of bestowing an angry tirade onto a class isn't a display of presence; I personally didn't respect many teachers or coaches that used this method. I was much more inclined to listen to someone that spoke with calmness, clarity, and with feedback that was specific and relevant to me or the group. So, how do we become one of these people that is able to communicate with efficiency, clarity, and purpose, even in the most challenging of teaching environments?

The first element of advice here is to demonstrate consistency with your routines of communication. There is no go-to winner here, and it really is for you to go away and experiment with several different methods, but you might use a blast of a whistle followed by 'stop stand still', or you might implement a countdown '3-2-1 and stand still/eyes on me'. Whichever particular routine you choose, if you use it consistently with a group over a period of time, you might even begin to see an element of conditioning taking place where pupils 'know the drill' and ready themselves for further instruction on hearing your consistently used command. This advice is particularly important when working with primary school pupils. There is a likelihood that their day-to-day classroom teacher will use consistent communication based 'attention grabbers'. As such, pupils will be used to reacting to a particular command in a particular way. Early application of a method can make your teaching life much easier. During my time coaching 'soccer' in the United States, we used 'Are you Ready?', to which the children replied 'I was born ready, Coach!' Now, this is unlikely to be the one to use for you, but you get the point!

Keeping with the communication theme, consider how you refer to your pupils. I am a huge advocate for teachers to work tirelessly to build up and maintain high levels of respect with their pupils. Take time to consider how you refer to classes as a collective, what is your go-to term? Are you happy using phrases such as 'Lads', 'Lasses', and referring to pupils as 'Son' or 'Mate'? Personally, I do not believe that these terms and this style are the most appropriate and professional methods to adopt, especially if working in a new school or with a new class. Might sound quite 'Old School' to some readers, but I commonly refer to pupils as 'Gentlemen' or 'Ladies', and some may argue equally that this could be inferred as derogatory or patronising. Essentially, the fundamental point being made is to consider your language; whilst not eradicating colloquialism completely, use it sparingly. Using professional language with classes will make a further worthwhile contribution to the development of mutual respect between pupils and teachers that will, in turn, support the development of a stronger presence in a lesson.

All the advice regarding communication methods can be completely discarded, however, if you are competing with anyone or anything else for the attention of your pupils. During lessons, you need to make informed decisions regarding the instructions you provide to pupils that prepare them to listen effectively. There isn't a PE teacher on the planet skilled enough to communicate to a year 7 class whilst they have a basketball in their hand (likely to be bounced several times per 10 seconds of teacher instruction), a badminton racquet within reach (likely to be 'twizzled' or used as a sword with their partner), or if there are several distractions within a 200-metre radius behind your teaching position. As such, consider instructions regarding how you would like your pupils to listen – 'Come in and take a knee', 'Place your racquet/basketball on the floor', 'Eyes on me please', before attempting to impart words of wisdom. Consistency of these forms of routine will also positively contribute to a more commanding presence within a lesson.

The dream combination regarding presence is to couple the advice relating to verbal communication with positive body language. Pupils buy into the overall package of a PE teacher. Different methods of communication are vital but considering how you stand, how you move, and your facial expressions can all support you in holding a presence within a lesson that is going to support pupils' progress. How can you expect your pupils to be energised and engaged if you look disinterested yourself? This is easier said than done, but park any external stresses or issues that may have arisen during the day and dedicate your energy to those pupils in your care for the next 50 minutes, 1 hour, or however long the lesson is due to run. Pupils often mirror teacher behaviour; if you enter the lesson looking like you cannot be bothered, there is a high likelihood that your pupils will behave in the same manner.

Linked to body language is considering your movement around a practical lesson. Circulating around pupils whilst they work displays an interest from you as the teacher in the quality of work that pupils are producing. Many early placement trainees can end up teaching an entire lesson from a 5m x 5m invisible square, usually located near their whiteboard covered in learning objectives or next to their lesson plan. Be prepared to move around a range of pupils in your lesson. A common observation of many PE teachers is that they will position themselves near the strongest performing pupils within a lesson, almost as if giving them an affirmation that their lesson is going well because the two county netballers are managing the passing activity with ease. Remind yourself that all pupils deserve your attention. Taking time to circulate and move around all pupils shows that you care, and can also help to eradicate any low-level disruption or off-task behaviour.

Finally, do not be afraid to practice when out of a lesson environment. Practice blowing a whistle in your own time – would you stop and listen to you if you were a year 8 pupil? Also, request for a lesson to be filmed. Once again, that player-cam idea that the camera follows and listens to you. How do you sound? How well does your voice project when it needs to? What does your own body language convey? Watching a lesson back with a mentor or colleague is always embarrassing, but it is such an incredibly positive and powerful tool in your development as an effective practitioner. You might cringe slightly, but it will provide you with the clearest of feedback possible of what it is like in one of your lessons. Ultimately, presence can be developed. If you have received critique relating to this in the past, do not be disheartened – take any advice on board and act accordingly!

Top 3 Takeaways!

1. **Be brave and record a lesson.**
   Watch it back and consider voice projection, positioning, commands used, and reflectively critique your delivery. This can be done by yourself, but is effective if conducted alongside a mentor or peer.

2. **Ask your colleagues and peers about your 'go-to' phrases.**
   Ask them to observe you and note down how many times you use your ' go-to' phrase in a lesson.

3. **Observe PE and non-PE teachers, and make a note of the commands used to address a class.**
   Take these away with you and try the ones you liked/that appeared effective in your next lesson.

Chapter Reflection

Helen Ostell, Former Director NEPSCITT and ITT Consultant. *@HelenOstell*

My experience in PE spans a number of years and a variety of roles:

- For nine years, between June 2012 and September 2021, I was the Director of the North East Partnership SCITT; a well-established, single subject SCITT, specialising in secondary PE. The North East Partnership SCITT is the largest provider of PE ITT in the north east of England, and one of the largest in the country. It has consistently been graded as outstanding by Ofsted (2005, 2009, 2013, 2022), and maintained top ten standings consistently in the Good Teacher Training Guide, as well as being identified as the top secondary SCITT nationally in 2013, and the best post-graduate provider in 2015.

- Prior to this, I worked as an Education Development Manager for the Youth Sport Trust, with a national remit for secondary PE; as a Partnership Development Manager working across a partnership of forty primary and secondary schools to develop PE and school sport; and as a Head of PE in two secondary schools, including one of the largest schools in the country.

- I currently work as an ITT Consultant supporting teacher training providers across the country.

From reading this chapter, and from my experience of working with trainee teachers and early career teachers, there are some key points that stand out as being useful pieces of advice for those who are trying to improve their classroom presence:

1. PE teachers must learn to modify their delivery and communication styles to suit the various teaching environments that they will find themselves working in.

2. Development of a classroom presence may happen at different stages for different practitioners. As with all elements of teaching, this is an aspect that can be developed through observation and effective reflection.

3. The notion of presence is much more multi-layered than 'a good old shout or rollicking of a disobedient class'. Pupils are much more inclined to listen to someone who speaks with calmness, clarity, and with feedback that is specific and relevant to the individual or the group.

4. Demonstrate consistency with your routines of communication.

5. Consider how you refer to your pupils and to classes as a collective. Consider your language; whilst not eradicating colloquialism completely, use it sparingly. Using professional language with classes will make a worthwhile contribution to the development of mutual respect between pupils and teachers.

6. Consider your non-verbal communication, for example: how you stand, how you move, and your facial expressions can all support your presence within a lesson. How can you expect your pupils to be energised and engaged if you look disinterested yourself? Pupils often mirror teacher behaviour; if you enter the lesson looking like you cannot be bothered, there is a high likelihood that your pupils will behave in the same manner.

7. Consider your movement around a practical lesson. Circulating around pupils whilst they work displays an interest from you as the teacher in the quality of the work they are producing. Be prepared to move around a range of pupils, not just the strongest. Remind yourself that all pupils deserve your attention.

8. Do not be afraid to practice when out of a lesson environment, and to observe yourself on video.

M

Making Moves

The competitive nature of the PE teaching profession dictates that you must give yourself the absolute best chance of making that winning impression on a potential employer or training provider. At each stage of the application process, the fundamental aim is to illustrate how you can be the perfect person and teacher for a school or ITT provider.

From my own personal experience, and from working with a number of trainees, the job, or training application process, can be highly stressful. The locus of control is, to some degree, taken away, with such important decisions regarding your future being in someone else's hands. There will be inevitable setbacks along the way – the perceived 'dream job' may come and go without success – and there might be situations where you aren't even offered an interview, after investing hours fine-tuning the application, but this is simply because so many people out there 'Wanna Teach PE'. This chapter outlines how you can maximise your chances of success at each stage of the process and, for those currently in employment, there are elements that you too can take forward into future positions within the profession, as you continue your teaching journey.

The likelihood will be that you will find a job or course advert,and the first piece of advice (and this might seem blatantly obvious) is take time to read the advert carefully. The employer or course provider will provide details about the particular role. Most importantly, this will allow you to make an informed decision as to whether this role is right for you, and will also prevent any nasty shocks when you cross the finish line and find out that, actually, the role includes 50% teaching timetable of a second subject, or that the role is only 2 days/week. Believe me, I've seen this first-hand where applicants have been left very disappointed when a detail (and massive details, at that) have been overlooked during the entire process.

Having read the advert, make some key notes regarding the role. Is there a sporting specialism indicated? Experience of teaching within a certain Key Stage? An emphasis on extracurricular activity? Involvement in primary schools or transition? Use the details from the advertisement as a checklist for your covering letter or application form. Ensure that you mention these honestly within your application, and support all statements you make with evidence. If possible, ensure that any evidence you use also outlines the impact that this had on pupils. Avoid floating proclamations of self-promotion. Be sure to sell yourself, but do so with all claims made with supporting evidence from your teaching, coaching, or employment experiences. In addition, be sure to get across your 'why'. Why do you want to pursue a career in PE teaching? What are the fundamental values that you hold as your core purpose as a practitioner of physical education? If you hold a strong passion for the promotion of healthy and active lifestyles in young people, be sure to get this across in your letter but, once again, do so with examples and evidence from your training or experiences so far.

During my time as a Head of PE, I have appointed several excellent professionals to our outstanding PE department. Through each of these processes, I estimate that I have read over 300 covering letters. The quality of these letters, I must profess, has been varied to say the least, but I have had the pleasure of reading many superb covering letters that have been rewarded with invitations to interview. The best covering letters make it very clear why that person would like a position of employment at that particular school, not just that they would like a position of employment somewhere, anywhere, please! As such, the takeaway advice is to make sure that your letter is bespoke to the school or training provider. If the school has a particular motto or strapline, use it in your covering letter. If the school's website has any information relating to PE or sport, explain in your letter how this excites you, how you would love to be part of the PE team, and how you feel you can become a valuable member of this team. It is obvious to staff responsible for shortlisting when a letter is completely generic. This paints a picture that a person is just throwing applications out there for any old job. Not only should the role excite you, but schools want to be excited by the opportunity to work with you too!

My final words of wisdom regarding covering letters and applications may come across as condescending – though I sincerely don't intend them to be – but, considering how many applications I have read that have fallen foul of this advice, I hope you will excuse me in mentioning this here. Please, take time to check through your application. Spelling is important. An application littered with incorrect spellings or poor grammar indicates to an employer that you do not take care or take pride in your work. When there are on average 30+ applications per PE teaching position, don't provide those who are responsible for shortlisting with an easy opportunity to 'cut' an application. In addition to spelling, please take care if you are working from a letter template. Whilst I implore all letters to be bespoke to the specific role and school, there will obviously be aspects from a template that you can use if applying for several roles simultaneously. But, before submission, please omit any mentions of other roles or schools. I have lost count of how many applications I have read where the applicant has blatantly just copied and pasted a previously-used covering letter, to the point that it has the name of a different school and headteacher throughout! Fundamentally, take care, and be proud that your letter illustrates to the employer or training provider that you are an outstanding candidate for the role.

Another stage of the process that can be overlooked is taking the opportunity to arrange a visit to the school. The main purpose of a visit is for you to ascertain whether the school feels right for you. This includes the commute, the facilities, the local area, the staff, and the students. In addition, the school visit can give you the opportunity to ask insightful questions of the tour guide, usually either a head of department or member of senior leadership. The school visit is almost like a research mission: specifics around curriculum, ethos, and qualifications covered by the department can all be ascertained during a school visit, and should be noted down following the visit, as notes of this nature can be used as excellent interview preparation. This said, the tour guide is not on interview! A bombardment of pre-prepared questions is not advised, just attempt to weave questions into the natural conversation during the tour.

Now, we can hypothetically presume that, as you will have followed the excellent advice from this book for the covering letter and tour, you have been successful in securing an interview day at a school. Commonly, this will consist of several activities, including a pupil panel, lesson observation, perhaps another tour led by pupils, and the interview. Let's start by focusing on the pupil panel. Many might argue that this is one of the more daunting elements of the interview day, but please try to relax. The pupils are simply trying to gauge whether they could picture themselves being taught by you. Now, this should not translate into you performing a stand-up routine, but you should aim to make every attempt at being engaging, positive, and inquisitive. That final point is crucial. Pupil panels often feed back that the candidate 'just talked about themselves the whole time'. Try to avoid this. Ask the pupils questions about PE and sport: what do they like? Is there an activity that they don't currently do that they would love to try? If you are inquisitive and clever with the questions you pose to pupils, the answers they provide could be used in the formal interview later that day. This can be evidence to a panel that you care about pupils, and their feelings towards physical education.

As a head of department, the lesson observation was always the most important aspect of the interview for me. From the perspective of the observer, they will be mentally placing you into a typical school day, and will make a judgement call as to whether your teaching style and delivery will supplement the ethos of the department. Fundamentally, they will be looking at whether you will be able to be left alone to deliver high quality lessons, causing minimal fuss. If that sounds blunt, then I apologise, but, essentially, it is true. I always sit back and think, 'can this person come in and deliver consistently in a manner and style that will suit our pupils?' If the answer is 'yes', then we are getting closer to bringing you in to be part of the team.

On receiving an offer of interview, you will hopefully also receive the title of your teaching activity. On receipt of the lesson title, consider any further information you may require to support your planning and preparation. Hopefully, you have heeded the advice earlier in the chapter regarding arranging to make a school visit, so many questions relating to facility space and equipment will already be fresh in your mind, but I certainly welcome any other questions that candidates may have regarding the lesson. If unprovided, request information relating to the group: assessment information, relevant SEND details on pupils, and anything else specifically around facilities or equipment that your visit didn't provide the answer to are all worthwhile questions that a head of department should be able to support you with.

Once these questions have been answered, the lesson preparation can begin. My advice here is to 'do simple well' as opposed to 'doing complex poorly'. The panel will want to see the fundamentals of your teaching practice. It isn't about iPads, a plethora of laminated resources, or a pyrotechnics display for the plenary; it is about getting across to the panel that you can teach a solid lesson that engages the pupils. Try not to confuse engagement with 'fun'. You are not applying for a Sports Camp Leader position – you are there to teach a concept, skill, idea, or element of theory or strategy effectively to the class you have been given.

If you can, in the build-up to an interview, have a run-through of the lesson on your teaching practice. I have had several trainees ask if this is OK, and I have always actively encouraged this. In addition, use pupil names during the lesson, in the first 10 minutes, get 4-5 pupil names in the locker and use them in your lesson when questioning or providing feedback. I've seen several candidates use name badges for pupils – a great idea, so long as its implementation does not eat into activity time. On activity time, keep the pace of your lesson high throughout. If you spot low level disruption, or a lull in the energy from the pupils, move the lesson on and keep up the flow.

Finally, on lesson observations, ensure your planning is detailed and bespoke to that particular lesson. Do not just pull a lesson off the shelf from your teaching file. This needs that love and attention that will ensure that you feel in control before, during, and after the lesson. I mention after the lesson specifically, as the final part of your day will be the interview, and the vast majority of panels will most likely include a question regarding your taught lesson during the day. They will be looking for you to reflect accurately and, by accurately, I mean, do your reflections align with the member of staff that observed the lesson? It is possible that a panel might ask you to reflect upon your perceptions of the content and approach you would adopt in a follow-up lesson. During these questions, do not descend into regaling the panel about the greatest lesson you've ever taught. Instead, be honest, and include a line about how you would teach the lesson differently in the future. This humility and honesty will be traits that the panel will appreciate favourably.

During the interview, consider everything you have learned throughout the process, from the information included in your letter (you may be asked to discuss elements from your letter in further detail), research you have conducted, comments from the pupil panel, and, as mentioned above, reflections from your lesson. Prepare also for the stock questions around safeguarding, behaviour management, etc that most schools will include on interview. Have an answer prepared, and make sure it is not generic but specific to the school. The interview panel wants to know about you, your beliefs regarding physical education, and your 'Why'. Why this career? Why this school? If your answers to the 'Why' are sincere, if they align with the ethos of the school, and if that panel can see you working with their pupils, then that beautiful, memorable phone call after the interview day might just happen, and your childhood dream is about to be realised!

Top 3 Takeaways!

1. **Review your CV regularly.**
   Check it today, does it reflect all your experiences, CPD and qualifications?

2. **Speak to colleagues and peers for support regarding covering letters and personal statements.**
   Some may even send you theirs to read through. Practice writing a covering letter and send it to your mentor for feedback.

3. **Conduct mock interviews.**
   School or course mentors will conduct practice interviews with you.
   Take feedback on board, address, and apply it in your next interview.

Chapter Reflection

Mark Tilling, High Tunstall College of Science Headteacher. *@HighTunstall*

Applying for and finding the right job is the most important thing for all potential teachers to do, and to make sure you align to the ethos and values of the school(s) you apply to is essential. This chapter outlines so many aspects that I would implore all potential applicants to follow.

What many candidates do not consider, which this chapter alludes to, is that you are also interviewing the school. As headteacher, I always tell candidates it is a two-way process and, therefore, from the very start of the process the school – and we endeavour to do this – should be promoting the positives about why you should be working for us, and what the benefits of being a member of staff are. If they don't, then do not bother applying, as staff don't matter to them. The paperwork provided by a potential employer is so crucial.

PE teaching is vital to the success of all schools. A well-run school will have a PE department that includes and drives performance from all, the most academic and the least academic. Make sure you have found out if sport is important – you can see that easily from social media and website postings!

The visit before application is probably one of the most important aspects of the whole process; remember you will be judged even subconsciously. Act as if you are on interview, as you can sway getting an interview or not at this stage. Those who turn up late to a tour, or don't show interest by asking lots of questions, already have a hill to climb, but remember not to act as if you know it all.

A CV is not important to me as a headteacher. In fact, if that were all you sent in, you would not be shortlisted. Be careful to make sure you complete the appropriate forms correctly, and keep the details sharp, as explained in this chapter.

Another really important factor reflected in this chapter is communication. When you get that offer of interview, or even the offer of a job, keep in contact with the nominated person in the school. What you do from the very start regarding communications with a school will quite possibly shape how you are seen well into the future.

The more I have learnt as a headteacher, the less reliance I have put on the lesson observation. I agree with the author in this chapter, keep it simple: it is relationships we want to see, not teaching skill. A good school will see potential and develop it. If they want the 'Ofsted' lesson, then maybe that isn't the place to be.

Yes, you may be asked to teach out of your specialism, but this is normally because of timetabling and staffing issues elsewhere. And besides, this can be a big plus for you, especially if your second subject sits within their culture and ethos.

Our biggest parts of the day are the pupil panel and pupil tour. In a good school, they will feed back to the interview panel, and will be very blunt. I have had pupils say to me 'they have no personality', and 'they didn't ask us anything, as they said they knew everything' – you can probably guess that those people did not get the job. It is because we trust our students who do the panels/tours that makes this part of the process so important.

In the interview, keep it simple. Don't over-complicate your answers. Remember, if you want to be at that school, the panel wants to hear from you why you want to be there: what excites you about being there, and what will you bring? In some form you will be asked, 'why do you want to teach at…?' If you want the job, make sure your answer is not, 'because it's near to where I live'. Good preparation will enable you to get the job you want – there are only so many questions that can be asked!

The most important thing, at the end of the day, is to learn from your experience, whether you have been successful or not. Ask for feedback, and don't let them fob you off – ask for details from every part of the process.

N

No Stone Unturned

When planning a lesson, leave no stone unturned. Consider everything. Mentally walking through a lesson from start to finish, from your perspective but, most importantly, the perspective of the full range of pupils in a lesson, can act as a mental dress rehearsal before delivering the real thing. There hasn't been a single PE lesson delivered in the history of the world that has followed the plan exactly, but the strongest lessons usually follow it pretty closely...

There are many approaches that can be taken, from a cognitive perspective, when considering the planning of lessons. Some practitioners find it useful to consider the ideal objective, or end product of a lesson, and then work backwards to ensure that the activities or lesson structure are able to support the full range or vast majority of learners to achieve the intended objectives. Other practitioners prefer to work in a chronological order when planning a lesson. Starting with a bell activity, then warm-up, then first activity, and so on. This method can be useful in aiding the flow of a lesson, avoiding 'down-time', and ensuring smooth transitions from one activity to another. Ultimately, regardless of the method, remind yourself that you are not teaching a mini-version of yourself. You are teaching a multitude of personalities, abilities, and interest levels in physical education. Your planning should reflect this throughout.

An aspect I feel obliged to reiterate is the importance of transition when planning. The flow and transition from one activity to another needs to be quick and slick. This isn't a coaching session at a local club – you can't buy yourself 5 minutes by sending the pupils for a drink or a toilet break. The avoidance of 'down-time' is crucial. Idle time between activities is when behavioural issues will occur, and disengagement will be prevalent.

Lesson flow and transition can be aided by minimising the organisational aspects of activities being used. When considering flow, the first 5 minutes of a lesson can often be the most crucial. A bell activity or routine for classes can provide you with the opportunity to prepare and set out any resources required for the activities you have planned. Pupil-led warm-up routines can buy you valuable time to prepare, so that you can spend the remainder of the lesson being a teacher, providing feedback, support and encouragement rather than just facilitating. One strategy linked to resource planning is for all activities within a lesson to be able to be delivered following this initial set-up period. Often, a 20m x 20m grid might need preparing (unless a kind head of department is forward thinking enough to have areas of this painted already) but, once this area is prepared, all the remaining activities can be performed in this space. Once again, giving you the opportunity to teach, rather than your attention and energy being more focused on resource management.

Lesson flow is also greatly impacted by the ease with which a teacher applies progression. The best progressions do not require an entire overhaul of resources, re-deployment of cones, or in-depth instruction – they are subtle, targeted, and work to engage the full range of pupils present within a lesson. Progressions are also most effective when they are organic and natural, when they are implemented by a teacher who has taken the time to step back and observe the pupils in action, before making decisions regarding moving pupils on in an activity. Progressions become least effective when a teacher moves a group on because the lesson plan states that, after 12 minutes, pupils will progress onto activity X. In addition, as you work with a group of pupils for an extended period of time, you will begin to appreciate when a certain pupil or small group of pupils might require more or less challenge to reach success. In this instance, as the remainder of a class continues to work on an activity, you can speak to an individual or small group and provide them with an additional problem or challenge to overcome. Similarly, you may remove a condition to support certain pupils too. Take possession-based activities within a classic invasion game environment; certain groups might require an element of movement with the ball before passing to increase success/hammer home the objective of teaching the importance of keeping possession. Equally, other groups may find this too easy, so an added stipulation of zero movement with the ball or a further condition to increase the difficulty may be required to push certain pupils. Once again, step back, observe, and interject when appropriate.

This fluent model of progressing activities isn't something that will necessarily be written on a lesson plan, but is an aspect that can be crucial in underpinning the success of a lesson. That said, information regarding pupils should be included within solid lesson planning. This does not need to be overly onerous or time-consuming, but simply a note to be aware that certain pupils might require more or a less challenge at a particular stage of a lesson. Within primary PE, be sure to utilise supporting staff members effectively. Teaching assistants are likely to be attached to a particular pupil or class. In my experience, TAs are more than willing to support as long as they are instructed, informed, and guided as to how their support can be utilised most effectively. At the start of the lesson, objectives should always be shared with pupils, but don't forget your support staff. Inform them of the objectives of the lesson, and how they can support a pupil or class to achieve these objectives.

It is also helpful to note specific motivations or things that seem to work with hard to reach individuals (e.g.: Harry loves anything to do with Manchester United). Once again, this becomes easier with experience but, in the early stages, this should be something that a training mentor or head of department should be able to provide support with fairly easily. Furthermore, be sure to investigate the information held by the school to support teaching, such as pen portraits of pupils developed by the SENCO, or relevant pastoral information from a tutor or pastoral team.

It is also important to remember that, when planning, less can certainly be more. This isn't referring to the amount of detail required on the lesson plan as, ultimately, there should be sufficient information for you to be able to deliver a successful lesson. Often, this can be a good starting consideration: in this lesson, what would success look like for all pupils? As opposed to lesson plans being almost too in-depth, just to pacify a mentor or make you look prepared. The lesson plan is your plan – it is for you. If you work in bullet points, use them. If you prefer images and diagrams, use them. If you aren't overly confident with sport-specific terminology, note it down. Ultimately, use the documentation to provide you with clarity and a clear sense of the flow to the lesson prior to delivery. The plan itself should serve its purpose in providing you with cognitive space that can allow you to focus on the live lesson unfolding in front of you, and the decisions you make on your feet to meet the target of progress for all.

In my experience, working within a secondary school and with trainees, I believe that I have seen or used well in excess of 50 lesson plan proformas. Often influenced by either the latest educational craze, or by a popular educationalist that is being supported by their way being 'the way'. This trend of differing and ever-changing lesson planning will continue long beyond my retirement from the profession; it is something that you accept as you move through your career and, whilst I can't provide you with 'the way' to plan a lesson, I can provide you with three general considerations that will aid planning.

The 'What'. Stand back and consider exactly what you are wanting to teach your pupils within a particular lesson. This will be underpinned by the medium- or long-term planning documentation provided to you by a mentor or head of department. It could be conceptual, in that you are given a broader idea or aspect of physical education to teach, and you possess the autonomy to design activities that will address this concept. Consider 'aesthetic movement'. This will constitute many different formats, depending on whether it is with Y7 or Y11, experienced dancers/gymnasts or complete novices. Applying the concept to the group is key. It could be narrower, such as a specific skill, tactic, or compositional aspect of performance that you have been asked to introduce, apply, or refine with a class. In both these cases, I believe having this idea of exactly 'what' success looks like in the forefront of your mind when planning will keep a lesson on track. It will ensure it is working towards the objective, as broad or narrow as this may be.

The 'Why'. This should be asked throughout the plan, on each and every inclusion of an activity, drill, or idea within a lesson. Ask, 'why have I included this activity?', and 'does it support my overall lesson objective?' If the answer is 'yes', for all pupils in a lesson, then include the activity in the plan. If the answer is no, or you are unsure, then omit this from the plan. Too often, trainees will shoe-horn in an activity they have seen online or observed elsewhere, even though it makes no contribution in supporting pupils to achieve an objective. Commonly, this occurs in the warm-up phase. 'That looks fun for a warm-up' will be the thought, yet the reality is that it is eating into valuable learning time and lacks that link to the bigger picture.

Furthermore, asking 'Why' can be much broader: does this overall lesson achieve the aim of a school, or indeed National Curriculum? Would this lesson design have engaged you when you were a child? Would it engage that pupil who loves their PE lesson so much to the extent that it is the only reason they've attended school on their PE day? Would it contribute to helping you win that battle with a pupil or class that isn't engaged in PE at all? Would the lesson work towards fostering a love for physical activity for the pupils? A range of questions to answer, and not all can be answered in a single lesson, but having these deeper questions in your mind during the planning phase can help you revisit a place in your thinking where you remember exactly why PE is so important to you.

The 'How'. This is where detail comes into play – the pedagogical processes and teaching styles that will maximise progress and learning for all pupils. How are you going to design activities so that they address more than the bigger 'What'; how will the overall lesson address the deeper questions of 'Why'; and how are you going to ensure fluency between activities, challenge for all ability levels, and make all of this fit into the allocated time you will have with a class, after changing time and the several kit issues and notes from home have been addressed?

The reality is, your plan is not going to meet the entirety of the 'What', the 'Why' and the 'How', but it will certainly give you the best opportunity to address them if you take time to give them consideration. Lesson planning is for you, no one else but, try to remember, a successful lesson is never just written on paper. The delivery, adaptations, interactions, twists and turns provided by a mixing pot of human beings, personalities and attitudes towards PE and your management of all of these variable will underpin successful delivery – but a solid lesson plan does help to mitigate these variables to an extent that will provide you with the aforementioned confidence to deliver to the best of your ability. An effective plan also reduces your cognitive load as the teacher, and allows greater focus on observing pupils during activities, and making those key, on the spot adaptations to support pupil progress.

I would not be able to conclude this chapter without one final consideration. All of the advice so far has focused on Plan A. The plan that, if no adverse event takes place, shall be followed, as this is the best possible lesson design for the pupils being taught. However, as many experienced teachers will be quick to remind you, it is vitally important to have a Plan B, also commonly known as the 'contingency plan'. There will be occasions, sadly too frequent in my experience, where planning and delivery is disrupted by a number of factors out of our control. Weather, examinations utilising the sports hall, staff absences and, most recently, a pandemic all mean that Plan A often goes out the window, and we are forced to resort to Plan B. My advice is to be mentally resilient in these instances: put the pupils first, put your personal pride or convenience second, and deliver a lesson that is as close to your own and the school's ethos around physical education as possible. This might involve the 'double up' scenario, it might mean sharing a facility, or even taking a class that you have never worked with before. Once again, try your best to put your emotions aside, consider the best interest of pupils, and work around the circumstances you have been given. Having a number of winning and readily accessible 'wet-weather' or 'Plan B' lesson alternatives in your teaching toolkit will serve you well throughout your career.

Essentially, with regards to planning, leave no stone unturned. Be prepared that, if something comes along that causes disruption, take a breath, put the pupils first, and do your very best with the circumstances you are given.

Top 3 Takeaways!

1. **Create a folder of contingency/wet weather plans – times that require a stand-in activity for larger groups.**
   Have it to hand and ready to go with short notice.

2. **Ask a mentor or colleague to use a stopwatch to keep track of activity time within a lesson.**
   Movement = Clock running, standing still = clock stopped. This could act as an eye opener with regards to transitions between activities, and time taken to share instructions.

3. **Ahead of future lessons, in less than 10 words, try to note down the fundamental objective of a lesson.**
   Revisit this at the end of your lesson plan. Do all activities work towards this objective; if not, ask yourself why they are included in the lesson.

Chapter Reflection

Kevin Tiller, US Based Phys Ed Teacher. Massachusetts Elementary Phys Ed Teacher of the Year 2015. *@PhysEdReview*

This chapter really gets down to the nuts and bolts of lesson planning. Just like an athlete mentally goes through thinking about what their performance would look like, so should a PE teacher. The 'What, Why, and How' is a critical step towards lesson success and implementation. The ability of the teacher to foresee, adapt, and make changes is also very important. The best lessons are the ones that keep each and every students' needs in mind, in addition to quick and effective transitions. Planning for the unexpected is also needed in the ever-changing school environment, when teaching space is utilised by a school event, or the weather is uncooperative. Be prepared to be Prepared!

Organise to Maximise!

PE teaching will often feel a million miles an hour. If you dedicate time and mental energy to organisation, before, during and after each lesson, it will provide you with more control, and will also develop you into a teacher that teaches, as opposed to simply an activity facilitator that supervises.

You are halfway through a Tuesday in late November, you have had two lessons already, you have three to go. You have been inside on badminton lesson 1 with year 7, then you were out on rugby with the year 10s, next lesson you have GCSE PE theory, then you have your tutor group, before taking year 9 girls health and fitness last lesson. This is all before your fixture away, 15 miles down the road that you have to be at by 3.45pm because the hosts do not have any floodlights, so you need to leave your school by 3pm. This will mean you will get back to school at about 5pm, back to your house by 6.15pm with all the rush hour traffic and this is just Tuesday! Your Wednesday is even more hectic, your next PPA lesson isn't until Friday last lesson!

Without organisational considerations at every juncture of your day, this workload is not manageable. Your practice will be littered with mistakes, you will overlook details linked to lessons, forget or not consider the logistical considerations along the way, and will most dangerously be doing your mental health and well-being no good at all. If you are organised, however, you give yourself the best chance of performing to the highest possible level whilst, most importantly, controlling your stress levels to the point that you can function effectively in work and enjoy your time away from school. Developing that early bird habit, as previously discussed, refers to the day to day dedication and rituals required to keep moving forward. In addition to the early morning ritual, time and energy must be set aside for clear thought and preparation when teaching PE. Think of the popular juggling/plate spinning analogies and you will be on the right lines.

Being organised is a multi-faceted consideration and is often supported by a practitioner getting into positive routines and adopting an almost rhythmic approach to their working practices. A routine that I cannot recommend highly enough is for practitioners to manage their own personal calendars effectively. Begin an academic year or placement by filling your calendar with key dates that require your attendance and involvement. CPD events in school, meetings, pre-arranged tournaments or fixtures: all of these should go in the calendar at the earliest opportunity. In addition, be sure to organise your calendar to include time for yourself. Any prior engagements or events in your private or social life should go into the calendar too – remember, successful and prolonged teaching careers are underpinned by ensuring practitioners make time for themselves.

In addition, ensure your daily timetable is organised, and make a note of the activities you are covering each lesson. This is different to lesson planning; this is a quick, go-to reference for you to use. I would also recommend making a note of the content of the previous lesson. It stops the eternal 'what did I do with this class last week' mental dilemma. Simply reference your calendar and your memory will be jogged sufficiently to put you in a solid mental space to deliver. Fundamentally, whether electronic or on paper, getting into a habit of using a personal calendar is invaluable. Personally, especially with the recent emergence of virtual or online meetings, I prefer to use an electronic calendar linked to my mobile phone. I also use the alert feature effectively to remind me of upcoming events, but I also use this to set a daily alert, simply entitled 'check your calendar'. This occurs every morning at a time just after I routinely arrive at school and reminds me that, before I begin any other task, just to spend a brief moment checking my calendar to get my head space and thought processes exactly where they need to be for the day ahead.

With your personal calendar routine well underway, acting as a safety net and comfort blanket rolled into one, lesson delivery organisation becomes the next major consideration. As exemplified in the opening lines of the chapter, PE teaching is a million miles an hour – as such, practitioners are always looking for methods, tips and strategies that will buy or allow themselves more time. Organisation prior to and during delivery can provide a practitioner with invaluable increased time at their disposal to teach, as opposed to merely facilitating an assortment of random activities due to disorganised lesson preparation and a haphazard approach to organisation during a lesson.

Prior to the lesson, get into that store cupboard and make those final checks that you have everything you need for the activities you have planned. It is no one else's responsibility if the balls have deflated, the bibs have gone missing, or if you do not have the required number of tennis balls. Grouping together all of your equipment prior to a lesson can make it easier for collection on your way to the lesson location. Also, and this may seem obvious, always request the services of pupils to assist with collecting equipment to take out for you, especially for outdoor lessons. Looking after your body and back is important too!

Once you are at your lesson location, buy yourself time to get organised, be it to display learning objectives (although, is this something you could have done prior to the lesson?) or just to get your equipment sorted. In our school, pupils are relatively conditioned to lead their own group warm-ups. Instilled into pupils from year 7, it is an expectation that pupils take time to warm themselves up, or for pupils to get straight into a bell activity. Get in and get going. Simple instructions that can be delivered in seconds, and act as a catalyst for pupils to be active as soon as possible. For example, in basketball lessons, I start every lesson by allowing pupils to shoot at a basket. This way, I can be preparing equipment and resources and, also, everyone loves shooting! An easy way to engage a class from the very start of a lesson.

Be sure to use this invaluable 2-3-minute window effectively, and have one simple question in your mind, 'What can I do now to buy myself time during this lesson?'. If you require cones to be laid out, use this time to do so, if you are going to use bibs, can you lay them out to be easily collected, can they be in coloured piles ready to go? If you are using balls, can they be out of the bag ready for ease of collection when required by pupils? Could a non-performer be utilised to support aspects of lesson preparation, if done so safely? All of these considerations will positively contribute to increased activity levels of pupils in your lesson, and allow you more time to teach, demonstrate, and provide feedback to pupils.

During the lesson, can you factor in subtle ways to keep on top of your lesson resources? Pupils collecting in cones used for an activity, or returning balls back to their bags, or any other resource-related management you can incorporate into your lesson and instructions. I often find that if I delegate specific tasks to sub-groups within a lesson, all to be done against the magical PE teacher's 10 second countdown, then this can be effective in minimising the need for a mass clean-up operation at the end of the lesson. These elements of transition between activities, groupings and equipment need to be factored into lesson planning. The benefits will be increased fluency within lessons, and more time spent on activity and learning.

Whilst the organisation of equipment is vitally important, and can be a contributing factor to the success levels of a particular lesson, the organisation of pupils is arguably a more important and crucial aspect when considering pupil safety. Organising the ways in which you would like your pupils to observe, receive instructions, and perform activities will all contribute to lesson success. When demonstrating, take time to think about how you would like your pupils to observe the demonstration. Is it important for them to sit down to aid focus? Can you organise them in a manner that is going to remove all possible distractions, to ensure that the focus is on the person or people performing the demonstration? For this point, consider the viewpoint of all pupils. Is the sun in their eyes? Is there something more interesting to catch their eye directly behind you or your demonstration? Do you need the class to place their racquet, bat, or ball on the ground, to ensure you are the focus of their attention? Do you need to bring the class in for each and every instruction? Does this harm the flow of the lesson? Instead, could some demonstrations and instructions be delivered from a distance, with pupils observing from their working area? Is a demonstration required? If so, can it be short and sharp, with the aim of supporting pupils whilst getting them active again swiftly? All these considerations are important, and should formulate your planning prior to lesson delivery, but should also be running through your mind as the lesson is progressing, taking the time (there's that word again) to observe progress and engagement and reacting accordingly.

Organisation and time have almost a reciprocal relationship when it comes to PE teaching. Giving yourself time to get organised prior to lessons, during planning and preparation, will buy you valuable time to teach during lessons. The use of a calendar, as previously discussed, will enable you to manage and apportion your time accordingly. On time management, do not take PPAs for granted. As tempting as it can be to use them as extended breaks, they are on your timetable to be used as planning and preparation time.

Mentally checking off responsibilities and tasks linked to lessons, fixtures, and other commitments is highly recommended too. Bookending your days with consideration as to aspects of your role that require organisation can also be useful, and provide you with that rhythm and routine your career will need. Before you leave in the evening, take that minute to check the calendar for tomorrow. Is there anything else I need to do before I go home, to ensure that home is for me, and not for worrying, work-related thoughts? Then, in the morning, start your day with that check through of the calendar to 'get your head in the game'. Remember, you are in the middle of the winter term, days away from your next PPA, another 5-lesson day followed by a fixture lies ahead – without organisation, not only will the pupils suffer, but you will too.

Top 3 Takeaways!

1. **Develop a habit of making your final act at work on an evening having a quick check through the calendar for the following day.**

2. **In the morning before school, take 10 minutes to devise a 'to-do' list.** When you complete a task, be sure to tick it off the list and stride forward with your day.

3. **Develop pupil-led routines that can support organisation during lessons.** A teacher should never collect their own cones!

Chapter Reflection

Mark Stewart, long standing colleague. *@HighTunstallPE*

As a current practitioner and a teacher of physical education for the past 7 years, I hope my reflection of Ben's words will prove insightful, achievable, and, most importantly, helpful in your pursuit of becoming the best teacher you can be, and ultimately make the job as enjoyable as it can and should be.

In my experience, your successes and failures, highs and lows, and the opinions of you, from staff and students alike, are considerably influenced by your organisational skills. If students know that you plan lessons and think about them, rather than frantically running around to complete simple tasks, they will pick up on it, and they will judge you for it, positively or negatively! As you will know, every day in school can vary considerably. Give yourself the best possible chance of being successful – for me, that starts with being well-organised.

Ben makes reference to several key points which I fully agree with: get in early – this doesn't mean standing at the front door waiting for the caretaker or site staff to let you in, we all have commitments outside of our job, but the second you walk through those doors, you are a professional, and there are people relying on you. Give yourself time to set up your lesson, check emails, liaise with colleagues, and ultimately breathe before you start. Arriving five minutes before you start work puts unnecessary pressure on yourself and others, which is something that ultimately you can control!

The chapter also refers to checking your timetable and calendar for the next day and, in some cases, weeks ahead. Get into the habit of checking this before you leave and, subconsciously, it will give you peace of mind on your drive home that you know what the day ahead has in store and, in the event you have forgotten anything, you still have an opportunity to rectify it.

My final reflection of this chapter is around student-led routines. As a trainee teacher and an NQT, you can fall into the habit of trying to do everything yourself. We've all been there, but hopefully by reading this book you will avoid the same fate. Students are your allies; they like to help and, when they understand it will increase their activity time, they will assist you in part of every lesson. Give clear, concise instructions, and know which students you should give jobs to. This particularly applies to who you give the balls to – a tip would be to carry them yourself until you know the groups. Again, we've all been there; it's a harrowing vision when you see 20 balls flying in every direction, and you are about to be observed on placement! Good luck on your journey – it's a rewarding career!

P

Physical Literacy

Nurturing physical literacy should be the underpinning aim of physical education. As a result of high quality teaching and learning, coupled with a rich, personalised and diverse PE curriculum, pupils should develop a commitment to being physically active beyond their school years. This is one of the most challenging yet most rewarding aspects of PE teaching. Can you contribute towards a pupil making a commitment to being physically active, now and for the rest of their lives?

You don't teach physical literacy, nor do pupils achieve a grade 7 in physical literacy, or receive a gold award from a governing body for completing a race or event with a particular time or score. This can, in turn, make it particularly difficult for you as a practitioner to quantify, in respect of a percentage of pupils in your classes, that you believe are making good progress towards their physical literacy development. It is crucial that you do not become too focused upon even tracking or classifying individuals as either physically literate or not, but the core values of physical literacy should be close to your ethos as a PE teacher. Having them at the forefront of your thinking during the planning, delivery, and reflective aspects of teaching is highly recommended. Does your practice provide your pupils with a range of positive and meaningful experiences that will hopefully instil a habit and commitment in pupils to be physically active, long beyond their school years?

So, what is physical literacy all about? The International Physical Literacy Association (2017) definition provides much opportunity for dissection and contemplation, with regards to the important yet not exclusive role that physical education teachers can play in the development and promotion of physical Literacy. The definition states that, 'physical literacy can be described as the motivation, confidence, physical competence, knowledge and understanding to value and take responsibility for engagement in physical activities for life.' Within this definition, whilst all aspects will be discussed with regards to the part we can play as physical educators, it is important to remember that it is an individual's responsibility, and free choice, as to whether they partake in a physically active life in PE lessons, out of school, and beyond school. Our role, in essence, is to give pupils a physical education experience that is going to increase the likelihood in a young person making that positive and lifelong choice to be physically active.

A key focus of physical literacy concerns pupil motivation. This can undoubtedly be one of the most frustrating and, at times, baffling aspects of physical literacy as, commonly, the motivation of a pupil is determined long before they enter the sports hall, gym, or playing fields. Often, you will be inheriting a pupil or class from a different teacher or primary school, meaning their previous experiences of physical activity and physical education can hugely impact their motivation to display a proactive attitude towards physical activity. In addition, young people are under your tutelage for a very small amount of their weekly lives, usually around 2 hours of a possible 148. When you consider it this way, it could be perceived that you are really up against it as a physical educator, battling against all of the other external factors, such as home life, body image, self-confidence, and previous sporting experiences, but this is not to say that the battle is impossible to win.

To be able to positively impact a young person's motivation to be physically active is one of the most rewarding aspects of the profession. Getting to know your pupils and classes is crucial. Observe their conduct, attitude, and competencies in lessons. Is there visible and audible engagement, energy, excitement? Does a class or even an individual respond well to the facilitation of a competitive environment? Are there classes or individuals that could be described as the opposite? Speak to the pupils, value their opinions, take time to reflect if there is anything that could be done to ultimately motivate young people to take more ownership regarding their physical activity levels. Through observation, and providing pupils with a voice, aim to balance engaging content with appropriate levels of challenge for all pupils. The feeling of satisfaction or success within a lesson will motivate the vast majority of young people to feel like this again and, as such, you will be igniting that fire in a pupil to take their love of physical education, and converting this to physical activity out of school, into some of the remaining 146 hours available every week.

Nurturing and improving confidence is also really important, and this is not exclusive to physical education lessons, but instead helping pupils become confident young people. This confidence, although not solely in physical education, is undoubtedly influenced by successes and positive experiences during their PE lessons. Success doesn't mean 1st place, PB's and school records; it is unique to each young person, and your role as a practitioner is two-fold: recognise, value and appreciate success in your lessons, and ensure that planning and preparation are conducted in the interest of creating successful opportunities within an environment that is safe for pupils' physical and emotional stages of development.

Recognition of success does not have to be overly onerous; it can be simplistic. It can be during a lesson, through quick-fire praise of a positive action, and ensuring that praise is bespoke and accurate can have a powerful impact on confidence. Furthermore, praise can be over a much longer time frame. This could be through recognition of a pupil's improved attitudes to physical activity – this might be demonstrated through skill refinement and improvements in fitness but, even more powerfully, this could be through recognising that a pupil is arriving to lessons with full kit, or demonstrating much more resilience during lessons. Taking a moment to share with a pupil that you are proud of these longer-term positive changes can be powerful, and have an immeasurable impact on their confidence. This recognition can also be delivered through a parental/carer phone call home. This illustration of care from a teacher is highly valued by parents, and will almost certainly result in a positive response from a pupil who will return brimming with confidence – a confidence that began in PE, but will more than likely flow into other aspects of life, including non-school related physical activity. A word of caution, however: make sure praise is meaningful, otherwise it can come across as condescending, and seeking and receiving praise can also become addictive, which may not be ideal in promoting longer-term sources of intrinsic motivation. It can be really powerful in helping students become more confident and motivated, but the next step is to make them intrinsically motivated and internally driven to seek their own improvement, and not reliant on external rewards like praise.

Often, the easiest aspect of physical literacy for PE teachers to grasp and apply is the focus around the development of pupils' physical competencies. That said, this can be overlooked if a rigid, sport-specific curriculum is in place. Consider rugby; PE teachers can become frustrated when a class is unable to pass and receive a rugby ball without a plethora of forward passes and knock-ons, but how often do the same PE teachers spend time with pupils working on throwing and catching? Athletics season arrives, and a PE teacher will return to the PE office to berate the underwhelming triple jump scores recorded by a particular class, but when was the last focus on delivery on running, jumping, balance and coordination? This isn't the place for a metaphorical curriculum deep-dive, but how often do you step back to observe the basics in your pupils? If all lessons across a year dedicated 5-10 minutes to focusing on the physical competencies listed above, the outcomes in your traditional sporting areas would naturally begin to improve. With regards to physical literacy, by developing these physical competencies, you are providing pupils with the foundations to follow whichever physical activity path they choose out of school. Without these competencies, you may be inadvertently providing participation barriers that could be detrimental to the overall health of a pupil. With relation to physical competency, teachers should think carefully about general (agility, balance, coordination or stability, locomotion, and object control), refined (starting, stopping, accelerating, jumping, landing, changing direction, sending, receiving, passing, shooting, throwing, catching, etc) and specific movement patterns (triple jump, spin bowl, javelin throw, lay-up). Do we jump straight into the specific movement patterns without an appreciation of the general and refined movements that are required to perform that specialist movement? How does the saying go? Run before you can walk?

Appreciation of the benefits of physical activity and movement principles is a further aspect of physical literacy. If a young person is provided with this knowledge and understanding of the benefits of physical activity from early years foundation stages, all the way through to Key Stage 5, they are more likely to appreciate it. With this appreciation, a pupil is more likely to make positive and conscious decisions linked to participation in a physically active lifestyle out of the school context.

This is where your role as a physical educator to provide pupils with knowledge and understanding is crucial. I personally interpret this aspect of physical literacy across three key areas: concepts, rules and health/wellbeing. These terms may seem broad, even vague, but I feel if a practitioner's delivery can incorporate these themes, their pupils are more likely to make progress on their physical literacy journeys. Key concepts across a broad physical education curriculum should provide pupils with a range of transferable tactics, ideas, appreciations, and strategies that will enable them to be informed participants or spectators in the future. To the same end, although I do not believe the delivery of rules to be an isolated entity, pupils should have an awareness of rules applicable to sporting contexts, to further inform their knowledge and appreciation of the activity once again. If not rules as entrenched within a particular sport, such as offside, footwork, or double dribble, these could be unwritten rules of etiquette, whose deeper-rooted meanings could positively impact a pupil's life, such as showing respect to others and congratulating opponents. The final health aspects are crucial, at a time when children's health is a global concern, there is a paramount importance in ensuring that pupils have a clear awareness of the benefits of a healthy and active lifestyle. Discussions and teaching around recommended exercise guidelines, diet, and long-term effects/benefits of training/exercise must be shared with pupils, as well as how being physically active is valuable in itself. This knowledge and understanding allows pupils to make decisions around their own health and well-being from an informed position.

Having worked in the same suburb of the same town for over a decade, I regularly cross paths with former pupils. I always ask how they are, and if they are still playing sport or being active. It isn't the academy footballers, county netballers, or regional swimmers that give me the greatest joy when they tell me they are still active. It is the pupils who enjoyed PE, and inform me that they are still playing sport for local teams or recreationally with friends, or indeed just ensure that they get to the gym several times a month, that give me the sincerest sense of pride. It makes me come away from these encounters and think to myself, 'well, we must have been doing something right'.

Top 3 Takeaways!

1. **Be sure to utilise pupil voice to dig deeper into motivating and demotivating factors.**
   Make a note of common themes, and discuss with mentors and colleagues to share best practice ideas to address/harness them.

2. **Consider including 'healthy tips' in your lessons: advice linked to diet, exercise, mental health and well-being.**
   Remember, you are a role model – your words of wisdom are sure to hit their target.

3. **Be observant during lessons, and be sure to praise and recognise pupils for their endeavours.**
   Appreciate the individual context of each pupil, and reward and praise accordingly.

Chapter Reflection

Dr Liz Durden-Myers, Senior Lecturer In Physical Education, Bath Spa University,
The University of Gloucestershire. *@LizDurdenMyers*

There are some great physical literacy myth busters in this chapter from Ben. I really like the way he opens with what physical literacy isn't, before explaining what he believes it to be, and how it informs his current practice. Within the chapter, there are six overarching themes that he discusses. I have summarised my take-aways from each one below:

1. **Positive and meaningful experiences and opportunities**

    Ben articulates how, essentially, our role as PE teachers is to ensure that all pupils receive a PE experience that is going to increase the likelihood in a young person making that positive and lifelong choice to be physically active. Key to achieving this is placing the children and young people whom you teach at the centre of your thinking during the planning, delivery, and reflection processes, and by asking yourself whether your PE offer and practice provides all your pupils with a range of positive and meaningful experiences that will create a commitment to be physically active, now and long after their school years?

2. **Motivation**

    Ben highlights how motivation levels differ considerably from class to class, and from individual to individual, including how their previous experiences can significantly influence their perception and motivation towards their engagement in PE lessons. This, coupled with the increasing competition for young people's attention, from distractions such as social media and other recreational activities, means that the environment we create in the relatively little time we have with them in formal PE lessons is crucial in shaping perceptions and motivations towards further PE opportunities and wider physical activities. Understanding your pupils, including what motivates and demotivates them, is vital in understanding how to ignite their passion for physical activity, both inside and outside of school.

3. **Confidence**

    Furthermore, nurturing and improving confidence can help promote engagement in physical activity, as well as helping to create confident young people, able to navigate a wide array of challenges that they encounter throughout their lives. Redefining what success looks like, and facilitating a range of opportunities for all to be successful, as well as rewarding effort, can be useful tools in creating an environment that builds rather than destroys pupils' confidence.

4. **Physical competence**

Ben draws attention to careful consideration and identification of key competencies required to be successful, paired with the right pedagogical methods to facilitate progress in these competencies. An awareness of general, refined, and specific movement patterns can help teachers understand how to pitch and develop competencies with physical activity for life in mind, rather than just sport techniques.

5. **Knowledge and understanding**

Imparting knowledge of fitness, health, and movement principles are also key in helping individuals understand the value and benefit of being physically active. Also, learning about rules and tactics can unlock more positive and successful experiences in sport and physical activity. Ben highlights the importance of creating knowledgeable young people, who can make decisions around their own health and well-being and physical activity engagement from an informed position.

6. **Engagement in physical activity for life**

Ben brings this chapter to a close by discussing the incredibly rewarding feeling of meeting a past student who is still active, and who reflects positively on your time together in PE. This is, after all, the true mark of a lasting legacy of a positive PE experience.

Ben has done a fantastic job of interpreting physical literacy, with real life examples of what this means for daily PE practice. Hopefully, with more physical literacy informed PE experiences, we can create a future generation who have a deep-rooted connection to physical activity and will reap the wide-ranging benefits associated with an active life.

Q

Questioning

Effective use of questioning can provide a real insight into pupils' prior knowledge and learning within your lessons. Questions should be used to allow pupils to cognitively process the activities they are completing, whilst giving you as the teacher the richest and highest quality information from the horse's (pupil's) mouth, to aid your live delivery and future planning.

Questioning is a skill within your PE teaching toolkit that will develop with time. In my experience, it is one of the weakest aspects of many trainee teachers and ECT's teaching, certainly in the early stages of placement and/or employment. I often feel this is because it is an element of teaching that is overlooked during planning. Lesson plans will classically include timings, drills, diagrams, and differentiation, but too often do not consider the potential questions that a teacher may skilfully ask during a lesson to guide, challenge, and assess pupils' progress. By planning and noting down several questions that may be used in a lesson, this will firstly keep them fresh in your mind during delivery, and you may adapt these depending on the pupil or lesson situation, but having a list of 5 potential questions to be used will also keep the bigger picture or question, if you will, at the forefront of your mind.

That said, yes, you will hopefully use the potential questions when addressing a class, small group, or individual, but there will also be the 'live' and on the spot questions that need to be asked during a lesson. These will come to fruition as you observe pupils' performances, engagement, and attitudes. Questions such as, 'How could you have done _____ even better?' or, 'Are there any changes you or the team could make to improve your performance?'. Essentially, guiding pupils to reflect and self-assess in a swift and effective manner can lead to further engagement in an activity. Question style is focused around ensuring that pupils are not able to reply with a low-order/one word response. You want the pupil(s) to articulate a response that is indicative of the pupil applying their experience or understanding of the lesson, topic, or thematic context.

If a low-order or single word response is given, be sure to probe and encourage pupils to provide more depth to their response. This is often achieved through follow-up questioning. Simple follow-ups include, 'How?', 'What makes you think that?', 'Why do you believe that to be the case?' or, 'So what?'. These questions are requesting pupils to justify and evaluate their choice of response, and pushing them to support their answer with evidence and reasoning. Posing questions in this way can ensure pupils are challenged, and can also promote a culture of self-discovery, independence, and a 'can-do' approach. All these qualities are beneficial to pupils in their out-of-school contexts, and clever use of questioning can show pupils the way instead of leading them down the path. Live questioning and interaction should be brief, so as not to significantly reduce activity time but, moreover, used as a metaphorical jockey's whip, giving those pupils an extra push and posing a challenge that will ultimately lead to improved engagement in a lesson. It is important at this point to emphasise that 'brief' should not be interpreted as 'rushed'. Pupils require time to process the question that has been asked before formulating a coherent, articulate, and relevant response. To achieve this, be sure to provide pupils with processing time. Pause, and wait for a response. The average response time allowed by teachers is around 1.5s. Could you respond to a higher-level question in less than 2 seconds? Probably not. So, please bear this in mind when working with pupils. Take time to research and observe colleagues or examples online of popular questioning strategies such as *bounce, think-pair-share, or snowballing*. Challenge yourself to try these in your lessons; be bold in giving them a go, and honest in your reflections afterwards. Which strategy worked, which didn't, and why? How will you approach questioning in the next lesson?

After several seconds, if a pupil is struggling, it will be likely that the go-to protective wall will be built by the pupil, the dreaded, 'I don't know' response. This isn't always indicative of a lesson, activity, or question being pitched too high, it can also be the result of a distracted, disengaged, or daydreaming pupil. As such, do not become disheartened, but consider rephrasing, simplifying, or lowering the difficulty of the question posed. Being persistent with a pupil before reverting to 'phone a friend', by asking another pupil the same question, can be more time-consuming, but will be beneficial to the pupil in the longer-term, with respect to confidence and self-fulfilment, on the production of an appropriate answer to a question.

There will be times when, no matter the amount of probing, pushing, simplifying, rephrasing, and supporting, a pupil will still refuse or be unable to respond to a question.

In these instances, a strategy known as bounce questioning can be used to great effect. Bouncing a question around a group is an effective way of ensuring engagement, as it keeps pupils on their toes. The initial response or non-response can then be bounced across to another pupil for further discussion, to provide an answer or an alternative perspective. Pupils become accustomed to this method, and are prepared for it if it is used regularly. Consistency with questioning methods and techniques can aid the quality of responses provided by pupils.

A common observation of trainee and ECT teachers regarding questioning are the safe approaches used. Too often, teachers will pose a question to a group and will ask for a show of hands (although be wary that many schools adopt a no-hands policy too!). Teachers will then quickly scan the group before choosing the high ability pupil to respond. Try to adopt an approach that ensures a range of pupils are questioned during a lesson. To ensure that a variety of pupils are used effectively, a differentiated approach to questioning will have to be used. A question that stretches and challenges the high ability pupil will be pitched too high for many pupils, and the question used for a lower ability pupil will not challenge the high ability. This aspect of questioning will develop with experience. Your knowledge of pupils will allow you to ask questions that are specific to certain pupils' levels of understanding and confidence.

It is at these moments during lessons that you should really consider why you are asking a question, or series of questions. Is there a point to a question being posed at a particular point in a lesson, or are you just asking a question out of habit? What are you going to do with the information you receive as an answer to a question? Will it inform future planning? Will the answer provided benefit the other pupils in a lesson? Too often, questioning is tokenistic, and produces low quality responses that merely waste time. Avoid this by planned and well targeted questioning, which is utilised in response to actions and behaviours observed in a lesson.

Questioning will also be a crucial component of classroom-based examination or vocational physical education. For it to be successful, it is equally essential that you get to know your pupils. KS2/KS3 academic information can indicate their ability, and allow you to target your questions in order to stretch and challenge all levels within a class. By knowing your pupils individually, you will also be able to apply relevant assessment criteria to the full range of pupils within a class. Do all pupils need to evaluate, justify, or critique a particular topic? Will they do this during an exam? If the answer is no, then this line of questioning is wasted on certain pupils. Lower ability pupils could be more suited to lower order, identify-style questions – target these effectively to build self-confidence, and further develop a growth mindset that builds towards higher order questions. Higher ability pupils often must evaluate and formulate multi-layered arguments around a topic or question. In these instances, bounce the question around the higher ability pupils in a class to encourage exploration of multiple points, as this will be expected of them during longer written response questions in an exam.

Questioning styles and strategies are one of the most valuable areas of teaching that I have made the point of observing in colleagues. During my ECT years, I purposefully went along to observe teachers in both classroom and practical lessons, from within PE and other subject areas. Watching experienced teachers punctuate their lessons with targeted and thought-provoking questioning gave me plenty of ideas to take away and implement within my practice. Some of these methods I still use to this day. Others were not for me. I highly recommend taking time to observe experienced colleagues with a specific focus on questioning styles. For me, observing how colleagues could extract richer and deeper information from pupils was fascinating. Earlier in my career, I was guilty of closed questioning that provided pupils with an opportunity to respond with lower order, single word responses. Taking time to watch talented colleagues in action provided me with questioning methods that would encourage further articulation from pupils in their responses, which not only stretched and challenged them, but also supported other pupils in the class, listening to a stronger response from their peers.

Observing colleagues can be particularly valuable if you are having trouble engaging a pupil, or group of pupils. Going to watch a pupil in a different subject area can provide you with alternative approaches to attempt, if you identify they are proving successful for the same pupil in a different area, or it might confirm your thinking that this pupil is the same when questioned in different learning environments. Either way, the observations will be useful to your practice.

Ultimately, questioning must have a purpose within a lesson. Tokenistic questioning, where it is clear that a practitioner is implementing questioning because they feel they have to, as opposed to using questioning to effectively check understanding or stretch pupils, is unproductive and wastes valuable activity time. The advice given in previous chapters around planning, getting to know your pupils, and inclusivity all underpin how effective your questioning can be. Questioning that is considered, inclusive of all pupils, and built upon a foundation of positive teacher and pupil relationships, is much more likely to produce responses from pupils that inform your delivery, whilst providing you with an opportunity to assess the progress of your pupils within a lesson, and across an academic year.

Top 3 Takeaways!

1. **Observe experienced teachers and make note of the frequency, timing, and style of questioning used.**
   Challenge yourself to use at least one questioning method observed in your next lesson.

2. **Aim to pitch levelled questioning to pupils within your groups.**
   Consider which pupils are suitable for deeper and more probing questioning, and aim to utilise this in a lesson in the near future.

3. **On your next lesson plan, be sure to note down potential questions that you might use at different stages of the lesson.**
   Following the lesson, reflect upon whether you used them, and how effective your questioning methods were.

Chapter Reflection

Nathan Walker, Lecturer of Physical Education at Plymouth Marjon University.
@NWalkerPE

Ben provides a thought-provoking insight surrounding the use of questioning in PE, and discusses some top tips throughout this chapter. As a teacher educator, I regularly converse with PE trainees about the use and impact of questioning in PE, and 'improving the use of questioning' is a common target for many trainees and ECTs. Understanding the different types and style of question, the range of strategies and approaches of asking questions, and finding the right balance or number of questions are all pivotal in the success of their implementation. Effective questioning can assist teachers in checking for understanding, providing appropriate challenge, and an opportunity to address common misconceptions – all of which are essential in ensuring that learning takes place. Within this chapter, there are some key takeaways that PE teachers can reflect upon and implement in practice, hassle free.

I have summarised some of my reflections below:

1. **The importance of planning your questions**

    Ben describes through this chapter that questioning is often something that is overlooked in the planning process, and illustrates how this is a fundamental error. The considered planning of questions (and expected answers) can help to ensure questions are used effectively, in line with the intended learning objectives. Although it is important to be flexible and adapt to the learners within lessons, having some key questions planned will help maintain a focus within the lesson, and help to identify the knowledge and understanding of the intended outcomes. Within your plan, it would be beneficial to consider: what questions you want to ask, and what answers you expect to hear; how you are going to ask these questions (directed, cold call, think pair share, discussion, snowballing, etc); when, within the lesson, you intend to ask the questions (starter, pitstops, interjections, plenary, etc); and how long you intend spending on the questions. This careful consideration will ensure that questions remain purposeful, engaging, and challenging.

2. **Observing expert others**

    Ben provides a nice practical challenge for trainees and ECTs looking to develop their questioning: an observation of an expert other, with a focused lens on how questioning is used within the lesson. Taking note of timing, frequency, and methods used might help provide inspiration. Reflecting on the observation, using at least one of the observed strategies in future lessons, is a simple but effective way of developing this area. I would also suggest that observing teachers in the classroom from other subjects can also be beneficial. Some of the best questioning techniques I have observed happened when I observed an MFL teacher in a KS3 Spanish lesson. Of course, some of the styles might not apply, due to the physical nature of PE as a subject, but there will be some golden nuggets that you could apply to your own practice.

Ben has provided some great tips and practical tasks that can be completed to improve the questioning that takes place within PE lessons, through the considered planning of questions that are created to challenge all learners, and observing expert others in practice; these simple tasks can enormously improve the quality of questions, without any drastic changes. Hopefully, PE teachers will reflect on this chapter and ensure that more time and consideration is spent on the careful planning of effective questions that can promote meaningful learning experiences in PE.

R

Resilience - Ready for Anything!

Resilience is crucial to a long, successful, and enjoyable career teaching physical education. People do, however, take resilience as a given – a trait that every teacher will and must have. This simply is not the case. The multi-faceted aspects of PE teaching, the emotions, the demands, and the stresses make being resilient a challenge, but not an impossibility...

As I have already said, PE teaching days run at a million miles an hour. The sheer number of decisions that you must make daily, as a practitioner, is remarkable, from kit issues to behaviour, lesson design, pupil interactions, parental interaction, staff interaction, the list goes on and on. Then, linked to each of these decisions, is emotion. Every decision you make will have an emotional response: pride, frustration, happiness, dismay, sadness, bewilderment, fear, once again, the list goes on. Furthermore, the thousands of decisions, and subsequent emotional responses you make, will be replicated five days per week, 40 days per term, over 250 days per academic year! Then, factor in extra-curricular to the daily mix. The logistics, time, and energy that an extra-curricular programme requires also chips away at the PE teaching armoury. The need to roll with the punches, dust yourself down, and be a strong-willed resilient person is paramount. But remember, you are a member of a team. The whole is greater than the sum of its parts. If you lack resilience, you affect the performance of the team and its members. Selflessness is an excellent quality for a PE teacher to possess.

This chapter was one of the main personal motivations for me when I was writing this book: to illustrate that teaching physical education is not easy. It isn't just throwing a ball out to a group of pupils and saying, 'Play!' It isn't just taking teams to fixtures in your favourite sport. It isn't just rocking up to lessons and winging it. Like teaching any other subject, it is bloody hard! You will be pushed, tested, and expected to deliver day in, day out, whilst physically and emotionally exhausted. If you are reading this and undecided whether it is the career path for you, I recommend you step back and re-evaluate sharpish.

Further experience volunteering in a school setting might be a worthwhile next step to clarify this decision in your mind. This isn't an easy option because you liked sport and PE when you were younger. This is a career path that requires full commitment to the young people in your care. Anything less is an injustice to the profession and pupils you teach. Taking all this into account, every day that you teach, learn, reflect, and develop is a true demonstration of your own personal levels of resilience – take pride in this and keep driving forward.

Controlling emotional responses to unexpected changes is an aspect of resilience that, whilst easier said than done, is vitally important to your role. Plans will be shelved or altered; fixtures will be cancelled; facilities will be taken away at short notice; someone in the department won't put the cones or bibs back where they should have done; these things will happen. Throwing tantrums, shouting, and waving arms around may feel natural, but it is wasted energy expenditure. In addition, you are a paid professional – pupils' and colleagues' perceptions of you will deteriorate if they witness your volatile reaction to, let's be honest, minor adversity. In these instances, consider how you control your cognitive and somatic mechanisms. The classic 'take a breath and count to five' response. Giving yourself that time to think and process adversity or change can be crucial, and is much more likely to produce a rational response, as opposed to actions taken instantly and without consideration.

During the initial stages of your career, you will teach lessons that do not go to plan at all. Having taught for a decade, I still have lessons that I coin, 'Absolute Shockers'. These lessons happen, and there will be many mitigating factors that have affected the quality of the lesson, many of which will more than likely be out of your control. A strong mindset or coping strategy in these instances is to focus on aspects that you can control. Control the controllables!

When a lesson does not go to plan, firstly, accept that this will happen during a teaching career. Take a moment to reflect on the lesson. If there was disengagement, reflect upon why. If there was poor behaviour displayed, reflect upon why, and the strategies you used to combat it. Once this reflection has taken place, put this lesson into a box in your brain, send the box down the river, and let it float away. The lesson is finished. It is done. It is time to move on. Lessons are never perfect, but you owe it to yourself to self-reflect and carry learning forwards into future practice, much the same as you would to try to outwit an opponent in competitive sport. A poor lesson does not define you as a teacher. Whether during your ITT programme, as an early career teacher, or an experienced practitioner, you will have taught many more solid lessons than poor ones – remember this and keep moving forward.

Put negative experiences to the back of your mind. Push them down the river so that you can maintain a positive mentality towards the wide range of challenges that PE teaching will present you with over the course of a term. A 'can-do' mentality is so important when teaching PE. Too often, I hear of PE teachers saying that they don't teach that sport or activity, and it is often due to a 'can't-do' mentality that can be so damaging to curriculum delivery and, ultimately, the experiences of pupils. In my experience, heads of department do not expect every teacher to be an expert at every activity they deliver on a curriculum. What they do expect is for PE teachers to actively address areas of subject knowledge weakness through research, seeking support from colleagues, and by being proactive. Does a mathematics teacher avoid algebra as it isn't their favourite area? Does a history teacher avoid the Tudors and Stuarts because they did not learn it when they were at school? No. The same applies in PE. Every PE teacher can effectively teach all parts of the curriculum. It is about displaying resilience and the desire to learn and develop as a well-rounded practitioner of physical education.

To this point, the rhetoric is very much to be strong, resolute, and keep moving forward like a sci-fi robot walking through a burning city in an action movie. This is obviously unrealistic in every scenario during every day. Moving forward for a PE teacher requires a support network built upon empathy and compassion. These people will hopefully exist in the same school, but perhaps from a different subject area. They hopefully also exist in your department, providing you with a subject-specific but true empathetic ear. A support network will be far more sincere and long-lasting if you reciprocate the support. Further to being there for colleagues and friends, their challenges, difficulties and approaches to these issues can provide you with an alternative approach to your own, comforting you in the knowledge that other teachers are experiencing the same challenges as you. As always, seeking support is not a sign of weakness. Help is out there; do not feel alone. Support networks outside of teaching exist as well, so be sure to talk to people you trust, and allow them to be your sounding board. 'Getting it off your chest' is often a crucial step taken by resilient teachers, but use this sparingly, as ranting too often can drain colleagues who will have their own challenges; be empathetic, and show your compassion for others too.

One piece of advice I have tried to follow closely throughout the most recent years of my career is to channel energy and focus into aspects of my role that I am able to control, as opposed to worrying about elements of PE that are completely out of my control. This is easier said than done, but a good mantra to remind yourself of in times of adversity. This advice is closely linked to the previous chapter regarding planning. If you are well prepared and have thoroughly planned, you have done your bit. If circumstances arise that require a deviation from the lesson plan or daily schedule, then pause, process the required adaptations, and proceed. You have focused on matters within your control – this mindset is crucial in developing self-efficacy and confidence.

To the same end, do not let change overwhelm, worry, or threaten you. Look to embrace it. There will be developments or advancements in the world of PE teaching that require you to move with the times. Remind yourself that yes, changing processes and procedures may require an increase in energy expenditure, but you have done this before. On the first day of a placement or employment role, you had to adapt to the ways of the school, or as directed by a course leader – you survived, coped, thrived and flourished, and you shall again. Change will happen, educational leaders are a driven breed. They will eternally be striving for ways that schools can be better. Sometimes, it will be by doing what they already do, but better. Sometimes, however, it will be by making radical and drastic change. As always, you can do this. Take a moment, evaluate what these changes mean to you, and drive forward positively. During my time at my current school, we have had numerous, almost regular, changes to our data and reporting procedures. One method is trialled, then another, and, whilst this ongoing pursuit of a better way is commendable, it can be draining to have to exert energy once again getting to grips with yet another new system. As before, in these instances, have a go yourself: are you able to overcome a particular challenge or change? If so, great, drive forward. If not, do not be afraid to seek support with the mentality that you are willing to learn, grow, and continue to develop.

Resilience is more achievable by those who display positivity. Be optimistic and face up to challenges, rather than approaching adversity with a negative and defeatist attitude. A healthy optimism often leads to teachers that are buoyant and teachers whom pupils want to spend time with and learn from. This positivity is contagious, and will rub off on your pupils. You will energise your pupils through your positive approach, and this will give you that boost, building your resilience. It is a reciprocal process in all aspects of PE teaching. You are a human being that will respond to different situations with different levels of emotion. But, if you adopt a mindset of 'can-do', of positivity, then the most daunting of challenges will feel more achievable than if you approach them with a pessimistic mentality. Remember your 'why', remember why you have chosen the greatest career choice in the world, and do your best – that is all anyone can ever ask.

Top 3 Takeaways!

1. **Look forward to the month ahead.**
   Make a note of any aspect that you foresee as a challenge, and seek support now. This forward planning will provide calm and clarity of thought.

2. **Count to ten.**
   Next time unexpected adversity shows itself, display a calm and measured response. Take a moment before considering your next action.

3. **Apportion time each week to address subject knowledge areas for development.**
   Spend 10-15 minutes researching and learning about an area of teaching that you would like to develop. Aim to put this research into action in lessons too.

Chapter Reflection

Ryan Ellis, Primary PE Teacher and Creator of the PE Umbrella Podcast.
@ThePEUmbrella

It's a real pleasure to share my thoughts and feelings on this chapter, particularly as resilience is something I've had to show on many occasions, although, equally, have sometimes found it hard to muster on the rollercoaster that is teaching. Through a career as a primary class teacher, PE lead, Primary PE consultant, and creator of The PE Umbrella, I've been fortunate enough to speak with practitioners around the world. Almost all would agree that 'resilience' is a life-skill that we would want ALL of our pupils to have when they leave school, and is almost certainly something we need to show through our time teaching the best subject in the world.

Resilience can be defined as 'The capacity to recover quickly from difficulties or setbacks'. As I'm sure we've all seen on the back of a global pandemic in our own pupils, resilience most certainly isn't a given, and is something that needs to be nurtured over time, just as it is for us all.

Yes, teaching PE is physically tiring, but nothing quite prepared me for the drain on my emotions that came along with it. As Ben states, it really can feel like a million miles an hour, and the sheer number of emotions that are thrown into this melting pot can take its toll. There will be times that we feel incredibly low, and bouncing back from this is essential. As humans, we tend to focus on 'negatives' in any given situation. This is known as the 'negativity' bias. If we teach a wonderful lesson, but had one pupil that behaved poorly, it's likely that we will focus on that when reflecting on the experience, even though there were multiple successes.

To that end, Ben provides some sage advice in reminding us to 'control the controllables'. Having the ability to pause, process, and then proceed in any situation is a wonderful superpower to possess as a teacher, and will strengthen over time, the more you overcome 'perceived' adversity. One controllable is our planning, and we must be proactive in preparing to deliver the best lesson we possibly can. However, this is really only ever a guide, not a script; you don't always know how a lesson will play out with 30+ unique pupils and personalities, all contributing to an ever-changing landscape. Situations will arise that test and push us to our limit but, no matter how difficult things may seem, we still get to choose how we respond. We choose how we react. This is something controllable. Once we acknowledge this, it becomes much easier to build up resilience and be kinder to ourselves.

I'm not naïve enough to think that you won't reflect on your sessions and potentially slip back into the 'negativity' bias (I still do), unpicking what went wrong or 'should' have happened. So, instead of framing your thinking in terms of 'if only...' frame it instead in terms of 'at least...'. Instead of thinking, 'If only the cones and bibs were where they should have been', perhaps try 'at least I got the equipment I needed for my lesson' or, 'at least my pupils progressed in their learning today'.

We choose the lens through which we view the world, and choosing a positive lens is a sure-fire way to build up your resilience and prepare you for the incredible world of teaching PE.

S

Social Media

To reward, recognise, and engage pupils, social media can be very powerful, and provide a connection between school and home. In addition, the collaboration and sharing of outstanding practice makes social media a must have in a PE teacher's toolkit. Use it wisely, safely, and productively to further refine and develop your craft.

Social media was initially, primarily used as a method of connection and entertainment; however, it has since diversified into an unmatched offering, pandering to all aspects of daily life, whereby anyone with an internet connection and a username has access to whatever they would like...for free!

From a physical educator's perspective, this can be incredibly worthwhile, and social media has provided untold numbers of valuable connections – primary and secondary, different region's approaches to physical education within a country, and how PE differs from country to country, to name a few. It has been the birthplace of thousands of incredibly positive interactions, which have ultimately resulted in delivery on the 'shopfloor' being enhanced for the benefit of young people.

Social media has provided the opportunity for PE teachers to compare their practice on a global scale. This creates an outward-looking perspective. Too often, practitioners can become 'safe', and adopt one of the most dangerous phrases coined within teaching: 'Well, we've always done it like that'. Social media can provide a window to an alternative, and I have often used it to win over colleagues that may have been sceptical towards an idea or concept. In addition to providing an alternative, it can also provide affirmation. If your ideas and approaches are being replicated in schools and by practitioners that you respect, this can furnish you with confidence in your practice that may not have been provided by colleagues from within.

Historically, certainly before the rise of social media, PE teachers had very little opportunity to share ideas. Time constraints, accessibility, insular approaches to PE teaching, and absence of organised meet-ups with other PE departments through 'Teach-Meets' or local School Sports Associations prevented any productive collaboration. Social media has connected PE people, and built positive networks and relationships that have ensured a progressive, positive, and supportive environment for PE teachers to work in.

Recently, #eduPE has seen an increase in the sharing of best practice, and I have witnessed an increase in practitioners sharing brief video clips of isolated drills and activity ideas from their own contexts. I personally believe that the reason behind the popularity of this style of sharing best practice is twofold. Firstly, there is no busier profession than PE teaching. Too often, the actual teaching can be well down on a jobs, to-do, or priority list, and this is fundamentally wrong. I believe that, due to the brevity of the clips, sharing in this style is providing a quick and easy method for practitioners to keep their delivery fresh, without an overly onerous research process being required. Secondly, the clips' visual nature allows the viewer to see the activity in action. From a personal perspective, this has really supported my delivery, as I have been able to watch a clip and think, 'That will work with this group, in this context, in this facility, with this equipment available, in this particular lesson.' In addition, clips can provide the visual stimulus to allow a practitioner's imagination to run wild. They also provide the opportunity for practitioners to take an idea and apply the adaptations required to meet a particular context, perhaps simplifying to suit a primary PE lesson, or complexifying to provide suitable challenges in a secondary PE context.

Further to collaboration is the overwhelmingly supportive nature of the physical education community on social media. There is a real sense of, 'we are all in the same boat'. This brings about a culture of caring and sharing with one another that ultimately benefits pupils through the freshness of ideas and resources made accessible. Historically, a textbook or website would address specific subject knowledge gaps, but could be a slow and, at times, tedious process. The PE community can swiftly locate the best contact and location for you to find the information you require and, commonly, people are more than happy to take time out of their day to support you. Be thankful, reciprocate favours in the future, and be a positive part of the #eduPE community!

In addition to sharing best practice and collaboration angles, social media is also a brilliant way to celebrate successes. As a parent of two young children, being able to gain a flavour of their school day through the medium of Twitter is so helpful for me to make that connection as a parent to my children's schooling. It gives me a starting point, or at least a prepared retort to the inevitable reply of 'Nothing' when I ask them what they have done at school today. It allows me to open with a 'I saw you did this today; did you enjoy it? What did you learn?' Within physical education, our departmental social media channels are popular due to their regularity of use, but also because of the positive feedback from pupils and parents. Pupils are aware that the channels are a way of celebrating their successes, within lessons and extra-curricular opportunities, whilst parents feedback that it keeps them in touch and provides them with the same readily available retorts to answers to, 'What did you do in PE today?'

The celebration of success through social media can be a great motivational tool for pupils. Recognition from a PE teacher through a simple post on social media to praise effort, outcome, or process can be the only positive recognition that a pupil receives in their school and personal life. It can also be a powerful way to show a pupil that they are more than capable, and that you have appreciated a pupil's endeavours as a teacher. This can be a fantastic confidence boost that may have a long-lasting positive impact on a pupil's confidence and attitudes towards physical education. On this note, social media can also be a way to recognise the 'unsung heroes' in a lesson. Those pupils that do everything that is asked of them, but fly under the radar. Taking the time to post about their efforts can have a positive impact on them and their engagement in future physical activity, in and out of school.

Social media can also be used as an extremely positive PR tool for a school. Quality of physical education and sporting opportunities remain very high on many parental agendas when it comes to deciding upon a school for their child. Positive use of social media to share best practice from lessons and sporting successes can be powerful, and have a real impact on the perception of the school within a local community. If you have a fantastic curriculum that engages its pupils, showcase it. If you have a thriving extracurricular programme, publicise it. Social media provides your department and your teaching with a platform to share and, using our own school's context, this has proven to be an invaluable recruitment, retention, and transition tool for the school.

Social media does have its risks and dangers. Protecting yourself and your pupils online is incredibly important. You are a professional; your online presence should replicate this. I have seen many teachers fall foul of what they are perceiving as personal usage of social media being deemed as inappropriate and unprofessional. Taking time to monitor your personal privacy settings is highly recommended. Sadly, too often, pupils, parents, and people you deemed as those you could trust can expose and share your personal content. The world of social media also moves at a rapid pace, with new trends and platforms emerging all the time. Stay vigilant, and comply with your school's E-Safety policy.

It is also recommended that your historic usage of social media is reviewed. Even with the tightest security settings, you cannot be too careful. As mentioned above, your online community, as much as you believe and hope, in the modern day cannot be trusted. If you approach it with this mentality, you will be fine, as sad as this may be. Prospective employers will look through your social media – even if this is ethically incorrect, they will. Photos of people drinking alcohol, fancy dress, comments you have made when you were younger; if all of these were viewed would they portray you as the young professional that is seeking employment in a school? If you have any doubt, delete the content and, once again, revisit those privacy settings, to protect yourself as a teaching professional.

We all love Physical education, it is our passion, and social media, used safely with your own personal quality assurance, is proving to be a powerful catalyst for positive reflection and change within Physical education. Surround yourself with an online PE community that aligns with your ethos and your personal 'Why?'. Continually reflect and implement its usage with pupils at the forefront of your thinking, and this can only be to the benefit of all.

Top 3 Takeaways!

1. **Consider the following PE accounts to follow on Twitter:**
   @WannaTeachPE (Obviously!) @PEScholar @PEGeeks @PEGeeksCorner @YouthSportTrust and many more!

2. **Conduct a self audit of your social media.**
   How does your online profile come across on all platforms?
   Do your privacy settings need tightening?

3. **Does your current school utilise social media?**
   Is this something you can drive or recommend to the powers that be?

Chapter Reflection

Tom Southall, Secondary PE Teacher and creator of the PE Classroom online platform. @PEClassroom

In the modern world, everybody spends hours and hours of their time on social media. For lots of people, this may be time wasted. However, by filling your social media contacts with the right kind of people, you will be receiving inspiration and teaching ideas every single day. All free of charge!

I highly recommend creating a Twitter account and following some of the hundreds of PE professionals who can help you on your own PE journey. By 'borrowing' ideas from lots of different PE teachers, you will be able to uncover what works for you in your school. Make sure you remember that there is never a 'right' way to teach PE, and ensure that you also bring your own ideas to the table when planning lessons. Teaching is very much trial and error so, if you see a new idea or resource in the Twittersphere, then why not give it a go.

In addition to 'borrowing' other teachers' ideas and resources, Twitter can also be a great tool for sharing your own lesson ideas, and asking for advice. Let others know about what has worked in your lessons, and ask for help with planning, assessment, or behaviour management. Take the resources that others share on the platform, but also share your own! There is no better feedback than one of your resources being 're-tweeted' and shared amongst the PE community.

However, be aware that not all of the teachers that you find on Twitter will be positive and optimistic. Unfortunately, some teachers will use the platform to discuss the pitfalls of teaching, and the problems that they experience with staff and pupils in their school. There is absolutely nothing wrong with looking for support, but be careful not to become a 'social media moaner'. Make sure that the time you spend on Twitter/social media is fortifying you with inspiration and energy. Fortunately, the vast majority of PE teachers use the platform to support each other, and to offer advice and encouragement.

When I trained as a PE teacher in 2011, I had the support of my PGCE cohort, and the teachers in my placement schools. Trainee teachers today have open access to hundreds of experienced teachers on social media, who have spent years perfecting their trade. Use this to your advantage!

T

Trust

Teaching is a profession built upon the foundations of trust. Colleagues trust one another to fulfil their role as part of an effective team. Parents entrust you to care for, support, and teach their children. Pupils trust you to guide them on a journey that will hopefully foster a love of physical activity, by sharing your passion for the best subject on their timetable…

Trust is so deeply ingrained in teaching. For me, when trust is absent, teaching is superficial, and learning will not be deep-rooted, or will be non-existent altogether. Pupils must trust your processes, your style, and believe in the activities being delivered. Trust does not develop overnight; it will take time and, with certain groups, classes, or pupils it will take much longer than others. Sharing the bigger picture of physical education,n or the curriculum being delivered in the school, can help pupils to visualise their journey within the subject. The bigger picture might consist of the entire school experience, the key stage, the academic year, the next unit of work, or just the next 45 minutes of a lesson. Sharing this with pupils can provide context and understanding of the purpose of a lesson, or even physical education as a subject. Remember, many pupils will have had poor or non-existent experiences of PE in the past, and it is important to ensure that all pupils understand 'why' PE is so crucial to them.

Sharing your personal 'why' with pupils can help pupils to 'jump aboard' with you on the journey. Share your passion for physical education: why do you teach PE? Pupils are often inspired by teachers sharing their love for the subject. People like to buy cars from car salesmen and saleswomen that are passionate about cars. People want to eat at restaurants where they know that the kitchen staff are passionate about a particular cuisine. The same applies to PE teaching; pupils want to learn from, and place their trust in PE teachers who love PE! In addition, pupils need to feel that you understand it from their perspective. This builds their trust in you as they feel that you appreciate their own personal context, and that you appreciate every pupil is different – every pupil is not going to be a future Olympian, and that this is completely fine. This will create an environment between pupil and teacher that is much more conducive to growth and development for the pupil.

In addition to demonstrating your passion for the subject, trust and respect from pupils will grow based on their perception that your passion for the subject is also illustrative of the care that you display with regards to your own ongoing subject knowledge development and depth. Please do not confuse this specific point with a misconception that you must be an outstanding 'decathlete-esque' performer across all areas of the curriculum – pupils do not expect a PE teacher to be able to demonstrate a back somersault, to the same level as their handball jump shot, to the same level as their discus throw. However, they do expect their PE teacher to have a deep level of researched subject knowledge, which will provide the foundation for teaching and learning to take place. Often, pupils can be sympathetic, and have almost been appreciative and understanding of some of my less refined practical demonstrations, some of which have received a round of applause – sarcastic – but a round of applause nonetheless!

Trust in teaching and, without getting too deep, in life, is often a reciprocal consideration. Within a PE context, for pupils to trust you, you must illustrate that you also trust them. Often a gradual process, built up week by week, on occasions after months or years of working with the same group, subtle changes in language and gestures that empower pupils and strengthen a positive teacher/pupil relationship can be implemented effectively. This trust in primary PE begins to be built from EYFS, all the way through their primary school journey. The interest you can show in a young pupil can be genuinely life-changing. Use of names, remembering interests, and interaction during play-sessions can all contribute powerfully to the development of a pupil.

With reference to language, can you carefully rephrase how you would traditionally instruct or request an action from a pupil or class? As opposed to, 'You will now set up the goals or bibs' could you say, 'Year 6, can I trust you to set up the goals and bibs so that we are ready to play?'. As opposed to bringing a group in to listen to instructions, explain to the group that you would like to trust them to routinely be ready to listen to instructions from their working area to increase activity time. Knowing when to tweak your language and instruction should be based on your instinct. Trust it. Your gut instinct will often guide you, telling you when the time is right to loosen the shackles on a class, or a particular pupil, in the interest of allowing them to flourish. If it doesn't pay off, take a moment, reflect, and be brave enough to continue to trust your instinct – it will be based on your experiences of the past, and guide you well in the future.

Subtle gestures that you make as a PE teacher towards pupils can also develop a trusting environment for learning to take place. Requesting a particular pupil, the unsung hero perhaps, to lead a class warm-up, carry in the bibs, set out the cones, or officiate a fixture or game aspect within a lesson can illustrate to a pupil that you trust them, as they will appreciate the importance (or perceived importance) of the request you have made towards them. Within primary PE in particular, this can be incredibly powerful indeed; you have the power to make a pupil feel like the most important person in the world! To many pupils, you will be a role model – some may even idolise you – and for this person whom they hold in such high respect and regard to place trust in them can be powerful. For some, this is the only time anyone trusts in them at all.

Further to pupils placing their trust in you, a reminder that you are also entrusted by parents to care for and look after their most valuable possessions. Communicating regularly with parents can build trust, and a positive relationship that will result in pupils feeling supported in their development within the subject, at home and in school. This communication need not be rosy and positive all the time. People trust people that tell the truth, and being prepared to share negative elements of a pupil's time within PE with home can also be powerful. In my experience, parents appreciate being 'kept in the loop': behaviours or attitudes displayed in PE may replicate behaviours that parents are finding challenging at home. Further to this, behaviours and attitudes displayed in your lessons may be completely alien or unexpected, when compared to how a pupil conducts themselves at home. Either way, communicating with parents with transparency and honesty, as difficult as these conversations may be, will have positive outcomes for the pupils. What would you like to experience as a parent for your children? Sometimes, taking time to reflect on this can help guide you.

As a PE teacher, you are also a trusted member of a team. A team that is striving towards an end goal, the delivery and embodiment of a school and/or department ethos. PE departments are very much like a weak-link sport; they are only as strong as their weakest section. This language and analogy may seem strong but, with respect to delivery of standards and expectations, everyone pulling in the same direction is crucial to consistency in performance, outcomes, and experiences of pupils.

This pupil experience should not differ greatly from teacher to teacher. If everyone in a team is fulfilling the departmental expectations, all pupils should have the desired experience from the subject. During your own schooling, your experience of a subject is likely to have been impacted by a teacher. Many times, this will have been positive. However, on occasions, this will have been a detrimental experience, and has likely shaped or altered your perception of that subject to this day. You will likely have had friends or peers that have a completely alternate perception of the same subject, and this can commonly be due to a specific teacher.

From a head of department perspective, I trust that all members of my team will teach with our departmental ethos at heart. I trust that the team will uphold expectations of pupils in all classes with all pupils. There is no greater frustration for myself than when I hear that a basic routine, expectation, or standard has been overlooked or ignored by a team member. This undermines the messages being delivered by the department, and can cause a damaging ripple effect for the subject within the school. 'Mr _____ doesn't make us get changed at the end of the day' or, 'Miss _____ doesn't make us take our earrings out' or, 'Mr _____ hasn't rung home about my lack of kit once this year'. Inconsistency leads to confusion and, ultimately, a damaging lack of trust in individual teachers, the subject, and the school. A timely reminder that PE is not the universe – it may seem it to ourselves – but we are one subject in a school, and typically account for just 15% of a timetabled week for pupils. We are trusted by senior leaders to apply school policy; PE should not be seen as any different to any other subject area, working towards the school's greater aims. In the most successful schools, everyone plays their part. From the headteacher to the canteen staff, from heads of department to the cleaning team – everyone is in it together.

Developing and maintaining an environment built upon reciprocal trust is the most secure, safe, and productive climate for teaching and learning to be effective, and for pupils to thrive within physical education. Proactively consider how you can build trust with all of your working interactions and your role will be easier and more fulfilling for all.

Top 3 Takeaways!

1. **Spend time with the head of department to discuss policy.**
   Ensure you are confident in how to proceed with regards to a pupil not having kit, refusals, injuries, contacting home, etc.

2. **Revisit the bigger picture during lessons.**
   Plan to share and re-address the bigger picture of a unit of work or lesson. Discuss the end goals with pupils; make them aware of what they are striving to achieve.

3. **Set aside time each week to contact parents/carers.**
   Build trust with all parties by demonstrating that you care.

Chapter Reflection

Jon Tait, Deputy CEO and Director of School Improvement at the Areté Learning Trust, comprising three large secondary schools and sixth form colleges in North Yorkshire. *@TeamTait*

Reflecting on my time as a PE teacher, I have seen thousands of students come and go who really needed us. Not necessarily because they wanted to be an Olympic sprinter, or a professional sports star, but for something entirely different – something they didn't even know they were coming to PE for. For many students (and I am sure this is the same in schools up and down the country) school is their safe place. School is a place that has boundaries. And school is sometimes the one place where they feel that they can trust somebody. Whether it's trusting someone to confide in them about something happening at home or, in this case, trusting someone so much that they will attempt a somersault together, with the guiding hands of the PE teacher helping them safely through that movement. Building trust with an adult is something we probably take for granted, and a basic requirement of human development when you are a child, but for some young people it is more difficult.

However, in sport and physical activity, we can really make a difference. By establishing firm boundaries and rules in PE and sport, together with applying those rules with equality, I have seen young people start to believe in 'the system' again. When you speak to young people and ask them what they find most frustrating about life, or school, you will often hear them talk about perceived unfairness – when other kids get treated differently, or when they feel things go against them unjustly. When this happens, they lose trust and respect for the rule makers and, more importantly, the rule enforcers. But, in sport, we have the ability to build up this trust with the young people in our care, as someone who is fair, who applies the rules of the game in equal proportion to everyone, and somebody who will give everyone the same chances and opportunities.

Sport can be a leveller of social class, as long as young people trust in you, and believe that you will provide them with the opportunity to stand shoulder to shoulder against their peers, irrespective of their postcode or bank balance. Once you've established that trust with children, and they know that you will not let them down, that you won't apply the rules to favour the advantaged, and that you will be there for them no matter what, then you have achieved something quite extraordinary. You may not only have achieved your objectives on your lesson plan, enabling them to execute a lay up or a tumble turn but, much more importantly, in life, you will have achieved your goal to make them believe and trust in someone else. And that, as I have come to learn over the years, is a far bigger achievement than any one good or outstanding lesson will ever provide you with.

U

Understanding the Context

Developing an awareness of context for a pupil or class is a vital aspect of planning and preparation. The context of prior learning, ability, confidence, and attitudes towards physical activity can all underpin progress on a pupil-by-pupil basis.

If you were looking to buy a second-hand car, you would more than likely be keen to see a history of its owners, services, and a proof of MOT. This analogy can be applied to PE teaching, when you work with a class of pupils for the first time. The reality is that the class is essentially second-hand to you. They will have worked with a different teacher, or in a different school and with it, their experiences of PE, their expectations and routines, will all differ to your own. In this instance, communicate with colleagues. Good departments will conduct handovers, hopefully in person but, occasionally, this might be in document form. In the absence of a handover, mentors or departmental leads will be happy to sit down and discuss the nuances of a particular class, but try to instigate this yourself – be proactive in sourcing this information. These discussions should hopefully paint that contextual picture that will help you from the very start to ensure that lessons are appropriately pitched and designed to engage pupils.

In the absence of, or in addition to, discussions with colleagues, be sure to take time to chat with pupils too. This links back to the chapter, Get to know your pupils, but be sure to dig deeper regarding their perceptions of physical education. This isn't simply an opportunity for pupils to criticise fellow teaching professionals, so be aware of this but, if you take the time to find out aspects of physical education that they do and do not enjoy, this can provide valuable information for you to take away; this will help you to embrace their positivity towards physical education, and be mindful regarding any negativity highlighted by pupils. Note the use of 'be mindful'. If negativity does arise from discussion, this does not translate to removing this activity, policy, or approach, but it will help prepare you to consider how you may approach these aspects in your lessons.

Discussions with pupils and colleagues can and should continue as a class works through a curriculum. Understanding pupils' experiences provides you with an appreciation of prior learning that has taken place. This prior learning is like the foundation of a lesson. Often, an appreciation of pupil experiences of KS1 and KS2 PE is worthwhile if working with pupils for the first time in year 7.

The activities, concepts, and content being built up by you as the practitioner will only stand upright if built upon this secure foundation. Too often, PE teachers can wrongly presume that classes have a higher level of prior learning. This presumption is founded by teachers making comparisons to previous classes from different contexts, or expecting their year 7 class to possess the same levels of deep-rooted understanding and passion for a particular activity as the teacher themselves. So, be cautious, revisit learning from previous lessons or even years, if required, and do your research on your classes – be informed, not surprised.

Developing an appreciation of the context that physical education holds within a school is also vitally important. Understanding how PE and sport are perceived by senior leaders in a school can enable you to align your specific approach and delivery style to meet the desired intentions of the hierarchy. Multiple external influences will guide the direction that senior leaders will want physical education to take. Also, don't stop there. What do other subject teachers think of PE? What do the support staff, governors, and parents think? Take the time to understand and change, improve, or maintain their positive perceptions of PE.

Intentions for physical education could be 'An utmost priority for all pupils, the importance of regular physical activity is appreciated by all staff, and there is a school-wide drive for all pupils to access high quality physical education'. This is the dream scenario; there is support from staff at all levels for physical education and activity, and you are entrusted to make this vision a reality. Sadly, but in some respects understandably, this is not always the case. Influences such as exam results, appropriations of resources away from PE, and historical perceptions of PE and sport from a school (we've always done it like that, aaargh!) can all mean that our subject is viewed from a different angle than we would desire.

This can be a tough balancing act. Staying true to your 'why' and your fundamental values towards physical education, and aligning with broader school perception, strategy, and direction can be challenging. My advice? You are employed by senior leaders that are directed by a governing body to take a school in a particular direction, and you are employed within a larger team. Appreciating the context of how physical education fits within that school, and applying your own beliefs, style, and personality to match this as closely as possible would be a recommended approach and, as always, communicate with colleagues – if unsure, request guidance, and perform your role as a valuable member of the team.

Consider also the demographic context in which your school is located. Appreciating local culture, traditions, and lifestyles can provide you with a deeper understanding of your pupils. Is physical activity a priority in the local area, or in the households of your pupils? The answer is not always an automatic yes and, in a class of 30, you will have a wide range of perceptions towards physical activity, and these perceptions will differ from your own. Conducting your own research that focuses on the sporting traditions, activities, and interests of the local area can be important. Certain sports/exercise habits are more prevalent in some areas than others. Use this information in two ways: to further harness a love for the big sporting interests of the area, but also be bold enough to introduce sports or activities that lack prevalence within a community. This can equally engage pupils, in that they will be able to try something new. You can provide that 'hook' for sport and physical activity that might have been missing. Furthermore, be empathetic and understanding of cultural differences in attitude towards PE and sport.

Spending time in the local area of your school is also often a worthwhile experience. Is there a prevalence of a particular cultural group in the area? Is there access to local green space? Do there appear to be high levels of poverty or deprivation? These aspects will all impact your delivery, and the engagement of pupils.

The socio-economic make-up of your school's local area will have a huge impact on your lesson delivery, and broader role as a PE teacher. If you are working in a lower socio-economic area, there will be a multitude of factors that will influence engagement, or even participation in physical education. Pupil diet and sleep patterns will impact energy levels: would you feel like participating in a HIIT session without breakfast, and on only a couple of hours' sleep? Having compassion for pupils is vital. Pupils living in these areas may also be experiencing a range of emotional stresses, stemming from their community. Due to this, participation, bringing kit, and feeling like being positive is likely to be low down on some pupils' agenda. Being aware of this is important, so that you can approach your lessons and pupil interactions in the appropriate, compassionate manner. In addition, for these pupils, there is a lesser likelihood of involvement in sport and physical activity outside of school. Lack of parental support/interest, and barriers such as travel, cost, and being a young carer all significantly impact involvement in local sport, and interest in sport in general.

Alternatively, your school's context might be the complete opposite to this, but pupils from high socio-economic backgrounds can bring a range of alternative pressures and challenges. High parental expectations around sporting and academic success can become added stresses for you to navigate as a teacher: 'Why hasn't my daughter been selected?', or 'What are YOU going to do about my son's below-expected progress grade?'. Once again, seek advice from colleagues about the best strategies to employ to temper expectations and high demands.

With a true understanding of context, you will begin to appreciate the true definition of 'success' as a PE teacher. Remember, for some, having the courage to change into PE kit is success. Running for 30 seconds without stopping is success. For others, it will be grade 9's at GCSE PE, selection for county, regional or international squads, but, with a greater understanding of pupils, the school, the area, and how physical education sits within each of these contexts, you will be able to recognise, appreciate, reward, and encourage successful pupils. You will also be able to tailor your lesson design and delivery to meet each of these contexts effectively. Research, collaborate, and communicate with pupils, colleagues, and parents to develop a true appreciation of exactly what constitutes success, and you too will be a success. The power you possess as a teacher of PE can be truly life-changing to so many young people, built on those solid, reciprocal foundations of empathy.

Top 3 Takeaways!

1. **If not required to anyway, go out on a break or lunch duty.**
    Observe interactions between pupils. Instigate discussion with pupils.
    Whilst building those relationships, you will be able to gain a feeling for
    their context and perceptions on the world.

2. **Request a 10-15 minute chat with the headteacher or a senior leader.**
    Gauge their perceptions of PE in the school. This will help align your
    practices with theirs.

3. **Be positive. Be passionate about PE.**
    Recognise contextual success from pupils, and go above and beyond in
    ensuring this receives the praise and reward it deserves.

Chapter Reflection

David Curtis, Faculty Leader of PE and Sport, Teacher of PE and AQA Examiner for
over 15 years. *@DaveCurtis81*

Understanding the context is so important for various aspects of a PE teacher's job. We are
in a unique position within schools where we teach all students, and get the opportunity to
work with so many of them outside of the classroom, and in extra-curricular clubs too. This
gives us all the opportunity to forge positive relationships, which is critical in becoming a
successful teacher.

There are some great ideas in this chapter to get the ball rolling. Developing your own
'class profiles' can be useful in terms of recording useful information about your teaching
groups, but getting to know them individually through conversation is the most effective
method to build positive working relationships. When you move around the school, say
hello, and smile at any students you walk past – this will make some of their days. The use
of student voice is critical for all PE departments, and this should be carried out at least
once a year with all students. It is important that students are engaged in the curriculum,

but it is also important that we push students out of their comfort zones and challenge stereotypes. With this in mind, use your student voice findings to tailor your offer, not curtail it!

When considering what sort of school to work in, I have always found it much more enjoyable when I have worked in schools that share my values towards sport. Whether considering a new role, or evaluating a current role, it is so important that you gain an understanding of the culture and ethos of sport in that school. This will help you shape the future offer, and identify some of the barriers and challenges you face. On this note, developing really proactive and strong club links within the local community will benefit all parties. Engaging with the local sporting community in the various schools I have worked with has really helped to drive forward both participation and performance across all ages. If you can understand the context of your school, and the pupils whom you teach, you are already well on the way. All the best, and appreciate how lucky we are to teach!

V

Variety is the Spice of Life!

There is the likelihood that a career in PE teaching will span around 30-40 years. This longevity is achieved by ensuring a variety in working life that engages, interests, and motivates you! Pupils will also benefit from teaching that is varied and delivered by engaged, interested, and motivated teachers!

There are a plethora of approaches to teaching PE, and that's such a positive thing that inspires me! Curriculum design, lesson structure, and teaching styles can all be implemented in different ways. Often, the approach chosen is dictated by teachers choosing the usual, regular, frequently trodden path that they know; they remember the direction that the path will take them, but the destination will always be the same, just like those people that go on holiday to the same place every year. The destination is lovely, and they enjoy the familiarity and comfort. By contrast, I have always loved to travel, explore, and see something new, and this is how the best PE teachers I have worked with have approached their teaching. They have been brave and tried new activities and approaches, and have reaped the benefits from a new-found invigoration in their teaching, and this has been received and rewarded by highly engaged and motivated pupils. During my career, this has often brought itself to fruition through the introduction of new activities within our curriculum. Movement away from traditional sports to new and less traditional/locally prominent activities has provided a challenge. The challenge has been to develop an understanding of the activity, then explore how this activity will work in a particular class context. This cycle repeats itself over a career, in different contexts with new roles, schools, and challenges, but it is what keeps people in the profession and supports career longevity.

Curriculum design, philosophy, and delivery all have a huge role to play with regards to their impact on pupil engagement. Fundamentally, the curriculum should aim to meet the needs of all pupils within a key stage, from KS1-KS5. The curriculum also plays a vital role in contributing to the development of physical literacy, whilst meeting the directives of a national curriculum that has the habit of changing rather frequently. Your role is to take a group of pupils on a journey through an academic year; roughly, this will equate to around 80 hours of lesson time. Without variation and originality, pupil engagement will undoubtedly wane. There is a fine balance to be found in the establishment and maintenance of routine, and varying approaches to delivery. Utilise foundations of activities and approaches that have been successful with groups in the past (revisit pupil voice, or conduct a new round to gauge a rounded concept of success) and use these to develop new ideas and ways to 'skin the cat'. This whole process will require your reflections to be frequent and honest, with concluding thoughts always referring back to how you can use your experiences to improve your practice in the future.

Do your research to consider different or new approaches to those used in the past. Take the time to read around the benefits of teaching strategies, such as Sport Education and Teaching Games for Understanding, to broaden your approaches. Take time to reflect upon how a new or different approach will work with the range of classes that you teach. A blanket implementation will not meet the needs of all your pupils. Tweak the broader ideas of new teaching approaches to address the unique context of your school and teaching groups.

A career in PE teaching is long and, thanks to recent changes regarding pensions, now even longer! The most successful teachers I have worked with have not been afraid to reinvent themselves, to look at new ideas that are out there, and push themselves to experiment and try new ideas. Trying something new that clicks with a class or pupil can provide a teacher with that unrivalled intrinsic motivation and 'buzz'. Being bold and brave, and having the gamble pay off, provides an indescribable feeling of self-assurance. These moments are crucial in a long career. They help to invigorate and engage you as a teacher, and it is only energised PE teachers that will invigorate and engage pupils.

I often observe lessons where a teacher will reflect that the pupils were flat, and the lesson lacked atmosphere. I am always sure to feedback that this is likely due to pupils mirroring the persona and energy given off by their teacher. Lethargic teaching, that merely goes through the motions, will lead to lethargic pupils that will also only go through the motions – it is that simple. The lethargic demeanour displayed by these teachers is often confounded by the observation that the content being delivered is the same: run of the mill activities and ideas that have been implemented year upon year, without productive reflection being applied. Seek alternative approaches and try new ideas. Be proactive in broadening your teaching arsenal by becoming confident in approaching a single topic from multiple angles. Take the broad concept of overload within invasion games. I have addressed this concept in Gaelic and American football, hockey, capture the flag, Danish longball, the list goes on.

This confidence will develop from experimentation, feedback from pupils and colleagues, and by bottling up that brilliant feeling of when you try something new and out of the ordinary and it comes off. You risked it, and were rewarded with a winning idea that will now be stored in your mental library of teaching, ready to be taken from the shelf when the ideal opportunity arises.

Take every CPD opportunity available. Tap into the knowledge and experience of colleagues, and be proactive in exploring opportunities to develop beyond your current school. One of the strongest trainees that I mentored always had a hunger and desire to learn and develop. At the end of each weekly meeting, they genuinely concluded each meeting with a question for me: 'Give me one thing that I could be doing extra this week'. Now, the balance here is remembering that teacher training years are full throttle anyway and, on many occasions, I responded with 'Let's just focus on the weekly targets first and go from there'. But I did admire the desire and drive that this particular trainee possessed. Later on their placement, I did put forward additional challenges, readings, research and considerations for them to work towards. It is no surprise to me now that this trainee has gone on and progressed to be a very strong practitioner, revered by the head of department in their current school.

If shadowing or observing teaching from a different subject area, I always recommend that a focus of the observations is agreed beforehand. This will encourage you to zone in on this aspect of teaching, as opposed to the observations becoming rather broad and general. In addition, I recommend a follow-up meeting to debrief after the observations that you have made. This will allow the teacher to explain in detail the reasoning behind decisions that were made during lessons, and will help you to understand the thought processes behind these key decisions and their intended impact.

Variety in your working life is instigated by you. A proactive approach to stepping forward for new challenges, projects, and opportunities is looked upon favourably by senior leaders. Furthermore, there is some wisdom in the old term from the north east 'Shy Bairns Get Nowt!' – putting yourself out there to be noticed is always a positive. Volunteering and offering your services to support others helps to display a willingness and a commitment to the whole school, whilst also opening doors and pathways in your career that you may not have realised were possible, or even existed.

It is becoming all too common for PE teachers to become insular within the department and subject. Development of an 'Us and Them' attitude towards other departments and areas within the school is not healthy for a cohesive, broader school team. Broadening your horizons outside of the subject can be great for your CV, and experiences undertaken should be documented to be used as evidence for pay progressions, internal opportunities within school, and external job vacancies, not to mention the sense of job satisfaction and better overall experience for the pupils. This approach demonstrates your versatility, ambition, and motivation to be the best member of school staff at the headteacher's disposal, and not solely a teacher of physical education. Taking time to shadow pastoral staff, leading on school trips, involvement in Duke of Edinburgh, or offering your services to mentor pupils not only help to demonstrate a willingness to be a team player across the school, but are also great for your overall development.

Stepping out of the PE bubble helps to provide an alternative perspective on pupils, teaching, and the broader functioning of a school. Observing pupils' behaviour in different subject areas and around the school building is a valuable process. It allows you to note commonalities in their behaviour, but also to steal (yes, steal, teaching is all about stealing ideas to improve your teaching toolkit; I suppose you could say borrow, but you don't give the idea back, do you?) their ideas, strategies and teaching methods. Link each new idea to how it brings about that focus and engagement, which you will be aiming to mirror in the classic PE environment with those same pupils.

Taking time to observe in classroom-based lessons is valuable, to be able to watch and learn from teachers more accustomed to working in this environment. PE teaching is so unique in that not only do we have to master several different teaching settings across a PE curriculum, but we also have to teach examination-based PE lessons in a classroom setting. It is important to note that these examination classes often attract more attention by senior leaders for lesson observations and performance management targets. Naturally, due to their entire teaching load being in this environment, other subject teachers will be able to display routines, application of seating plans, and questioning methods that PE teachers don't get to practice as often.

In addition, be willing to utilise your PE network to observe the approaches and ideas being used in other schools. Request a period of observation, work experience, or simply a brief chat with teaching friends working in schools of a similar demographic to your own. For a broader or alternative perspective, connect with PE teachers in a completely different demographic, or even country to your own; exploit the wonderfully diverse world of #EduTwitter and #EduPE. What do they find to be a popular approach to teaching a certain curriculum area? Are they facing the same challenges with the same groups linked to engagement with physical education too? Pose your specific questions that you need to develop, and enhance your practice further. Ultimately, surrounding yourself with varied approaches to physical education is going to provide you with a broader and deeper understanding of the subject and its challenges. Equally as important, be proactive in ensuring that you vary your practice too. Keep yourself fresh and current. I have been teaching for over 15 years, and still look to try new ideas as a means of personal challenge; this approach, I believe, is crucial in ensuring a successful and enjoyable career teaching PE.

Top 3 Takeaways!

1. **Request time to observe in other subject areas.**
   Take the positive aspects of delivery and reflect upon how you can use them to improve your practice within PE.

2. **Within the next week, try something new: an activity, method of taking the register, a warm-up.**
   Be bold and have a go. Reflect on how it goes, adapt if required, and move forward.

3. **Be proactive in your own professional development.**
   Find the courses and webinars that will benefit you.

Chapter Reflection

Christian Fallick, teacher and school leader for over 12 years working in a wide range of schools around the south coast of England. He is currently an Assistant Headteacher responsible for teaching and learning, teacher development and CPD. He has been an educational consultant for PE supporting schools with teacher development, assessment, and curriculum design. *@MrFallickPE*

'I love teaching because every day is different'

I often reflect on this statement when speaking to colleagues and trainee teachers. Teaching allows students and staff to experience new and exciting challenges together, and we are very privileged to share this journey with our cohorts and local communities. We are at a very exciting stage in education, and the PE landscape is changing and evolving to the challenges we currently face. Low participation rates in boys' and girls' physical activity must be tackled, and this can only be achieved through new and relevant initiatives that build confidence, happiness, and a lifelong love of moving. This mindset and approach needs to be modelled by highly qualified, passionate, and enthusiastic teachers who embrace the culture of 'trying something new' in lessons to grow and foster independence and resilience.

Ben summarises the importance of variety very well in this chapter. PE should be at the heart of every successful school and, to be successful, you need to be forward thinking, and foster a culture of bringing new sports, challenges, and teaching practices into curricula, and after school provisions. Thankfully, as a profession, we are moving away from just performance in PE lessons and, as a community, PE can offer much more for our young people. Ideas for you to reflect on should be based on fundamental movement patterns, physical literacy development, leadership, and team development through the wonderful vehicle of Sport Education. Ben also highlights the importance of self development and growth, looking for new opportunities, and working with expert teachers across a school. If you are able to make this a priority for your own development, and your school can support this, I guarantee positive outcomes for all stakeholders involved.

Within this chapter you will have to reflect on the process of your own identity as a teacher: maybe you are an ECT, or a very experienced senior leader who teaches PE. Over time, you will observe cycles of 'in vogue' practice. Fads will come and go although, thankfully, due to the increased amount of research in teaching, these are becoming less and less relevant, and we now know what makes a successful learning experience through our knowledge of cognitive science. Personally, I believe the key here is to share, network, and find out what works well for different staff, schools, and departments. Every school has its own eco-climate; however, it is best practice to see the bigger rainforest around you. The only person who is responsible for your development is you, and therefore you must invest in yourself.

Finally, in schools there are many different roles you can explore over time. Each role brings different challenges and experiences. I have worked with teachers who are still thriving with 30 years of experience, and I often ask them for advice for new teachers. The same message I get every year is 'try something new'. This is such an important message, and one I continue to stand by in my own career.

Enjoy the chapter, and remember how lucky we are to do this job.

W

Wet Weather!

As PE teachers, we are superheroes, make no mistake. We have super powers, able to impact the health and well-being of pupils up and down the land. One super power not in our armoury, however, is the ability to control the weather. Within our control is planning ahead for inclement weather, and other unexpected adversities, so we can keep the train moving forward and not be derailed by variables beyond our control.

Now, I must admit, wet weather is an aspect of teaching that I have adapted my approach towards over the years. From a coping perspective, I tell myself that this is fine, it is a result of reflection and subsequent adaptations in my working practice. The reality? As I have grown older, I feel the cold a lot more than when I was younger! Joking aside, I do back my current stance regarding decisions made towards teaching in poor weather. Fundamentally, the environment of the lesson needs to be conducive to pupils making progress within the activities/concept/curriculum area being covered. If the weather does not suit a certain activity area on a certain day, I have no problem with deviation from the lesson plan to deliver an alternative activity that is going to be better served to address the core principles or ethos of our subject, to foster a life-long love for physical activity. It is also worth being mindful that being cold and uncomfortable are not the emotional memories we wish for our pupils to associate with PE, especially in younger pupils within KS1 or KS2 just setting out on their physical activity journey. If the environment has the potential for these emotions to arise, once again, there is no real issue in shelving original plans and moving to the contingency or back-up plan.

From this point, the question arises, what exactly constitutes 'cold' and 'uncomfortable'? In this respect, once again, you will have to apply context to the situation. This chapter is not providing teachers with an excuse to cancel all outdoor lessons when the temperature drops below 10 degrees, or when a single droplet of rain hits the grass! The group of pupils participating in the lesson and their nature should be at the forefront of your mind when making any decisions linked to whether the planned outdoor lesson should or should not take place. If unsure, speak to the departmental lead or line manager, and be sure to follow any activity or facility risk assessments to make sure that you are covered to teach the planned activities in the conditions presented to you.

Take a step back prior to the lesson: is this lesson safe to go ahead as planned for all pupils? If the answer, when looking through the original plan, is no, consider the adaptations required to ensure, first and foremost, safety, then engagement of your pupils. Adaptations may involve modification of activity, change of venue, or shelving the plans altogether. Do not perceive this as failure; you will find over the duration of your career that deviation from the lesson plan is unavoidable. It is about taking changes, often at late notice, in your stride, and using initiative and positivity to make the best out of each situation for your pupils.

In colder conditions, and in PE lessons generally, of course, keeping activity levels high is crucial. Considerations around the amount of questioning, class discussion, mini-plenaries, and 'down time' should be factored into planning, along with management of equipment and resources to ensure fluent lessons, with encouragement of moderate levels of physical activity throughout. In addition, avoidance of static performance of skills and static roles within games is important to ensure heart rates are kept high, and pupils remain in a comfortable state to participate. There shouldn't be any occasion in any PE lesson that a pupil queues or waits for their turn for more than 10 seconds and, in certain outdoor conditions, I would recommend that this timeframe is shortened further.

Queueing doesn't just exist in line drills. Goalkeepers in football and netball are effectively queueing (waiting) for involvement. In colder conditions, are goalkeepers or other rigid roles and positions necessary? Could lesson design be adapted to include smaller sided games to maximise involvement? Taking football specifically, are goalkeepers ever really required in a lesson? Now, we call this 'goalie when', and I'm sure you will know your local version of this. In the north east, it is called 'Mergies', but I've heard of it referred to as 'rush goalie', or 'fly keeper'. I digress, but hopefully you are grasping the general thread. Adapt lessons to ensure that activity design and differentiation lead to every pupil being able to access as much activity time as possible to avoid the conditions even being noticeable.

A further factor that helps to take pupil thoughts and feelings away from the less than pleasant conditions is the energy and enthusiasm displayed by you. I am a firm believer that pupils often mirror the energy levels displayed by PE teachers and outside, in wintery conditions, this becomes even more important. Crank up the volume and praise for pupils, and reiterate how proud you are of pupils that are demonstrating the energy and commitment towards their learning that you wish all your pupils to strive towards. If you are standing, shoulders hunched, hands in pockets, commenting on the cold, and looking disinterested, expect a similar vibe displayed by pupils. Furthermore, consider your appearance on the cold, winter days. Now, this is always a contentious point amongst PE teachers – for me, it's about balance. By all means, if it is cold, teach in a coat, but to be stood there like the Michelin man with multiple layers, a hat, scarf, and long-johns on, whilst pupils are outside in shorts and t-shirt, I don't think seems equitable.

An additional element to consider here is the rigidity of kit policy in colder conditions. When I teach rugby in the winter, I permit pupils to bring in additional/different items of clothing away from the school kit list. This ensures their comfort and is permitted on the condition that pupils work hard and are committed to participating fully in wintery conditions. This is something to discuss with the leadership structure within your school but, for me, is allowing a 'skin' or base layer going to be so detrimental to compliance with kit policy or performance within PE? In my experience, it is not.

On the topic of clothing across PE teaching in general, it is always good to have something else in your locker. I have fallen foul of this many times. Caught by a flash heavy shower during lesson 1 that leads to soggy boxer shorts and socks for the remainder of the day. I've also peered out of the PE office window many times and decided that trainers will be fine on the grass, only to walk out with a class to find out that the local area undoubtedly had torrential rain overnight, unbeknown to me, and has left the pitches like marsh land. Too late to turn back with 30 Year 9s in tow, trainers nobly sacrificed, but sadly caked in mud and moisture for the remainder of the day. Accessibility to spare kit is not only vital to the day-to-day running of a PE department for pupils, but also essential for PE teachers too. Spare socks, footwear, even underwear are all highly recommended to be items packed into the work bag of a morning.

All this said, especially in Britain, on some days, the elements will get the better of any worthwhile physical education teacher, and this will be clear from the outset. Double up lessons with more than one class coming together in the same working areas are inevitable. On days like this, indoor facilities become proverbial gold-dust. Undoubtedly, bickering/bartering/intense negotiation will ensue between the faculty members to decide which groups go into the sports hall and which groups must squeeze into the drama or dance hall. I also appreciate that, in many school settings, there may not even be a sports hall and, during exam season, a wet weather lesson might mean that there simply is no indoor facility available at all. As mentioned, many times throughout this book so far, yes, these situations are far from ideal, but they happen. Often, these situations arise with little notice but, in any case, there is not the time or need for arms to be flailed, or for whinging or negativity to be seen. It is time to display that you are a valuable member of a team, and that you are willing to roll your sleeves up and get stuck in.

The curriculum plan is likely to go out of the window, but the main aim for these types of lessons is to go with activities and ideas that maximise activity time and engagement within the parameters of the facilities, equipment, staffing available, and with pupil safety at the forefront once again. Taking note in a journal, or at least mentally, of the approaches adopted by experienced members of teaching staff in these situations is highly recommended. The more you find yourself in a situation such as the 'double up', the more you understand the activities and styles that work best, that get close to, or achieve the widespread engagement you are after. Be sure to also note down the organisational techniques adopted when working with large groups. Time taken to sort groupings or equipment is even more of a premium when trying to control larger numbers. Work smart. Prepare equipment, arrange working spaces, and be sure to communicate the broader plan with colleagues (if available) so that the proverbial singing from the same hymn sheet takes place in beautiful harmony, as opposed to disjointed freestyle battle.

Ultimately, in these instances, and throughout the scenarios broached in this chapter, keep on your toes. You must embrace late change with positivity (easier said than done) – dealing with the unexpected is such an underrated quality to have as a PE teacher, and this becomes easier when the ideas you have up your sleeve are tried and tested over time following review, reflection, and feedback from all concerned.

Top 3 Takeaways!

1. **Make sure you pack a spare kit for yourself in the morning.**
   Spare socks in particular are invaluable!

2. **Always be observant of your pupils, especially during colder/wetter conditions.**
   Gauge engagement, and adjust plans if required.

3. **Always have pupil safety at the forefront of your mind and planning.**
   Ensure risk assessments are reviewed, utilised, and referenced ahead of all lessons delivered.

Chapter Reflection

Francesca McEvoy, Lead Teacher of Physical Education, Beacon Academy, Cleethorpes. *@FrancescaMcEvoy*

'Wet Weather'... We have all been there, glorious sunshine on the way to work, and lashing it down by 9:15am! When reading the above chapter, much of it resonates with me as head of department in a mainstream secondary school. I will further discuss three areas: the curriculum, teaching and learning tips, and climate culture.

Let's start with the curriculum. Can the outdoor lesson be transferred to an indoor space? You may answer yes, and be blessed with the perfect indoor space. However, what if you're delivering long-jump and don't have an indoor sandpit? Let's accept that the lesson won't 'look the same', and put on your creative hat to teach the fundamentals. You may have gymnastics mats, and can still teach the techniques of a jumping event, ensuring that the children are still learning. Many sports offer alternative equipment for indoor delivery, which is always worth exploring. With bigger groups, we make the decision to 'double-up'. We deliver benchball across four badminton courts, perfect for mass participation. We keep it exciting by using different equipment on the courts (netball, tennis ball, rugby ball, and reaction ball). Courts are conditioned with rules, e.g.: passing the rugby ball with the correct technique, allowing curriculum recall and transfer of skills. Non-participants officiate, or are in charge of organising fixtures and recording results. Everyone is involved.

I agree with continuing to deliver outside (where safe), which brings me on to teaching and learning tips. Rule #101 of wet weather: avoid the children standing still at any point. Rule #102: lead with infectious energy! A tip would be to use changing spaces at the start and end of the lesson for instructions and plenaries. We must deliver differently outside. I circulate through the class, drip feeding them with information and differentiating tasks, making them either more challenging or accessible, to increase movement. Continuously praise and use the behaviour policy to give out lots of rewards. 'Teacher talk time' should be reduced to a minimum. Also, consider gathering in small groups to deliver instructions. This will keep you and the children moving and, most importantly, warm. This nicely leads me on to talking about kit.

As I like to say, 'there's no such thing as bad weather, only bad clothing', and my colleagues kindly remind me that this is not true…hurricanes! I would not go outside inadequately dressed, so nor should the children. The age-old argument of uniform policy vs engagement is at play here, and I strongly believe that we can all be more flexible. We offer an array of kit, including leggings, school branded jogging bottoms and hoodies, and 'skins' to encourage responsible decision making from the children. During cross-country, we encourage the wearing of hats and gloves. In our department, we have banned the 'F' and 'C' words…it is not what you're thinking…freezing and cold! Instead, we only use fresh and crisp. You would be amazed at how hilarious this becomes when your Year 7 cohort become Year 11 and they humour it along with you! We now have a culture of academy staff using these alternative words too!

To summarise, the core values of any PE lesson: keep them moving, learning, and having fun. And remember, you can only control the controllables!

X

Xtra-Curricular!

The clue is in the title; this will involve work and time that is extra to the delivery of the curriculum. Often unpaid, time-consuming, and energy-sapping, but vital to broader engagement in PE, and a crucial step towards developing lifelong sporting and physical activity habits in pupils...

In my experience, the most successful PE departments and PE teachers are those that place importance on and dedicate commitment towards their extra-curricular programmes. Once again, the nature of the programme will be dictated by the context of the school. This will range from high expectations and focus on performance and results, and the extra-curricular programme acting as an advert for the school, to others using programmes to address accessibility barriers to pupils, and provide opportunities for the development of health and engagement in exercise. There is also a likelihood that many schools will be a hybrid of both and, in all settings, strong departments will be sure to continually reflect upon their extra-curricular programmes to prioritise an approach that has the greatest positive impact on its pupils. Regardless of the motives behind extra-curricular activity, be prepared to demonstrate your commitment to the school by working with the team to offer the best possible programme for your pupils, and mentally remove 3pm as the end of your working day. You will see teachers from other subjects jumping in their cars and heading out of the gates at this time but, for PE, this simply isn't the case, as some of the most powerful relationships between pupils and our subject are developed after 3pm or, in some cases, before 9am.

During a placement as a trainee, or during your infancy working in a new school, my advice is to conduct your due diligence on extra-curricular and its fit at that school. As a head of department, I am always looking for new members of the team to provide additionality, and a point of difference, to our extra-curricular offer, whilst also providing us with the potential to broaden the opportunities for our pupils. After ascertaining the current offer provided by a school, get out there and speak to people. Being proactive by offering your services to your head of department will always be looked upon favourably. This may involve supporting a larger element or area of the programme, with high participation and a number of competing teams, or to address a coverage gap in the programme that your area of expertise could address. That said, you may also be called upon to work in areas out of your specialism. This can be daunting, but also a great baptism of fire, and an opportunity to showcase your versatility whilst developing your subject knowledge. In this instance, be honest, speak to colleagues if you are unsure, but be prepared to display a willingness to be a valued member of the broader team, and the output being generated by the PE department. In my personal experience, I joined a prominent rugby union school, despite being brought up with rugby league. I had to learn quickly and, due to the size of the rugby union programme, I had to get involved through necessity, to ensure we met the large demand from pupils. This was one of those aforementioned baptisms of fire, where I had to learn quickly, and apply the basic knowledge acquired from my RFU Level 1 swiftly, but the whole experience helped shape my practice and approach to extra-curricular sport and physical activity.

After conducting your own research, and especially in light of potentially delivering activities out of specialism, be sure to note any local clubs that could be willing to create a link between themselves and the school. Schools possess the dream customer/participant base that local clubs will be keen to access to promote their club and sport. This can be a reciprocal partnership, beneficial to both parties. Schools can benefit from resources, facilities, and coaching support from clubs, whilst the clubs are able to promote their out-of-hours sessions to pupils. Further opportunities for pupils to make physical activity a daily habit can only be a positive for all.

Use meaningful pupil voice to actively and continuously ensure that extracurricular programmes are meeting their purpose to engage young people in physical activity. I hope that all 21st century PE departments are able to create an extra-curricular programme that engages all of its pupils, not just the 10-20% who are active in community sport already. As such, pupil voice can be a powerful tool to shape delivery and design of extra-curricular. Focus around potential barriers, and strategies that could be adopted to address them, should be included. Also, listen to ascertain whether there are activities that aren't offered that pupils would enjoy.

A reminder that pupils also commonly vote with their feet; every few sessions, review and reflect upon factors that could be affecting attendance. Advertising, scheduling, familiarity, and broader access all impact attendance;be proactive in addressing these issues, and aim to maximise consistent participation. Once participation is consistent, there will be a likelihood that involvement in fixtures will follow. This could be intra-school, with matches/ events arranged between houses, tutor groups, or on a more relaxed, recreational basis, or it could be in the form of arranging fixtures with local schools on a competitive or friendly/developmental basis. I am a firm believer in the benefits to the school but, most importantly, to the pupils, when opportunities to represent a team are provided by PE departments. The teamwork, cooperation, camaraderie, and pride that can be developed through structured competition is unparalleled, and can provide that 'hook' or consolidate engagement within our subject.

The prevalence of competitive fixtures will more than likely bring about a mild headache, or even severe migraine from time to time but, even during the busiest periods, take stock and reflect upon your 'Why'. Recognise and appreciate that involvement in school sport to some is the absolute highlight of the school week, and keep striving forward to provide these opportunities for pupils. During these busy periods, organisation is vital. I would strongly recommend the development of a fixture checklist. The checklist should be visible in a planner or workspace, and should provide a reminder of all the elements of organisation that are required for a successful fixture or event to take place. Risk assessment, online paperwork/trips pack, venue, officials, travel, cover, communication to parents/carers, to mention a few, but taking time to mentally review each aspect involved is vital, not only for your own development, but also to ensure everything is covered ahead of a fixture.

As mentioned, fixtures involve communication to parents and carers. Ensuring that parents receive detailed information to provide confidence in you acting as Loco Parentis is vital. In addition, it is important to ensure home has the information they require to be aware of their child's whereabouts, and that they are safe. Unfortunately, school sport can also lead to the worst elements of parental involvement. Parents can be great, volunteering and supporting teams and individuals brilliantly. However, there can be interactions brought about through extra-curricular activities that can prove challenging. The parent of the pupil that is not selected for a team, the parents of the pupil that is prohibited from playing for school due to external club commitments, and the parents that feel inclined to pass on their sporting 'expertise' to you.

During all parental interaction, remain professional and calm. When returning phone calls to discuss difficult aspects, such as the pupil not being chosen for an event or match, preparing notes, or even a pre-written script – this will help you to focus on the key elements you wish to discuss. If you are unsure of the best way to respond, consult your department, line manager, and pastoral team linked to the pupil; they might be able to provide further context prior to making contact. From my experience also, even though it may be a more daunting experience, endeavour to make contact verbally, if possible. Email replies can appear insincere, and language can be interpreted differently to how you intended – a phone call eradicates ambiguity, and allows for open and fluent discussion.

A further element to extra-curricular, away from the regular weekly activities, are trips and excursions. Once again, truly memorable experiences for pupils that are often coined as highlights of an academic year or entire school experience. If you can volunteer as a supporting member of staff on an excursion, get that hand up. It will be a great experience to shadow trip leaders to understand the processes involved in taking pupils out of school safely. Once you feel familiar with the 'on the day' processes, be proactive and look to plan your own trip. Experienced colleagues will be willing to take or talk you through the risk assessment, letter, finance, transport, and trip launch procedures. PE-related trips should look to further enhance learning that takes place within the curriculum, or look to exist in the absence of a resource or curriculum aspect at the school. The pride that can be felt in leading an experience that a pupil would not be able to access without your hard work and dedication is a great feeling. You will be creating an opportunity that pupils will value and, in turn, respect you for bringing that opportunity to them.

Extra-curricular has provided me with some real career highlights. From winning trophies and attending national finals, to seeing that disengaged pupil find their 'hook', and watch it remain in place for years, eventually leading to pupils finding their sporting love that continues into adult life. I have also been lucky to take children out of their town and overseas for the first time in their lives to ski resorts, sports venues, and innovative areas of the sports industry. Only you will truly appreciate the behind the scenes effort, but the outcomes can be truly magical. That said, you are paid and entrusted by the hierarchy in your school to teach. Your teaching should always remain a priority ahead of extra-curricular, but being able to maintain teaching performance to a high level whilst providing incredible opportunities for pupils is a sign of an outstanding PE teacher. Continually develop your teaching craft and practices, whilst gaining extra-curricular experience in your early years, and you will be provided with a foundation on which a long and successful career in PE teaching can be built.

Top 3 Takeaways!

1. **Develop an extra-curricular checklist for fixtures.**
   Team selection, communication with parents, travel, insurance, risk assessments, facility booking, etc. Work your way through, and tick off as you go.

2. **Explore potential trip venues that can enhance a curriculum and engagement from pupils.**
   Offer to lead or support on a trip in the near future.

3. **Utilise pupil voice.**
   Dig deep into the activities and structure that will engage pupils. Use this feedback to design an attractive and inclusive extra-curricular programme.

Chapter Reflection

Hayley Wood-Thompson, PE Teacher and Head of 6th Form, Football Homophobia Hero Award Winner 2022. *@HWT_PE*

I cannot explain how important it is for new PE teachers to just get stuck in. Do not limit yourself. Say yes to that level one course in a sport that scares you; say yes to gaining your mini licence; say yes to running that district or county side one Saturday a month.

My most memorable moments of my time as a student were when representing the school in various sports teams, or taking part in school trips and experiences. It is these moments that have made me who I am today, not the standard of my school education. I was really lucky to attend a school with a large, thriving PE department, which was central to the school. A specialist 'sports college', when these were a thing in the early 2000s. It was what I got up for every morning, and is the inspiration for my 'why' now.

Those experiences provided me with so many learning opportunities, and enabled me to develop such close relationships with the PE staff, who I am still so inspired by today.

As a teacher, my career highlights include the bonds made with students, taking them on national cup runs across the country, giving up weekends and countless evenings to attend tournaments and events, and watching them evolve as a team, grow in confidence, and overcome challenges. I am still so full of pride and emotion thinking about some of those epic wins. Knowing that the time invested in this group of students has led to professional contracts being signed, and national and county representation. It is not always the big moments though; some of my fondest memories include watching an unlikely student suddenly 'get it', and having their whole world turned upside down. I will never forget taking a student who was in care on a plane for the first time on a school ski trip to the USA, and watching his eyes open to the world. Giving up your time is so valuable, which you may not realise when you are tired or busy, but there will be little reminders as the years go by, as to just how much of a difference you have made: bumping into a former pupil, receiving an email or a thank you card years later, or watching a pupil represent their country with their parents. Sometimes, the experiences and opportunities you can offer will provide a far greater opportunity for learning outside of the classroom than you can provide in it.

Don't forget how important your role is; as teachers, we are in the most privileged position to help shape the lives of our young people.

My takeaways!

1. SAY YES!

2. Explore options for school-club-links to help provide opportunities for students outside of school hours. This may also help you in-school, with special taster sessions and coaching opportunities: 'PE add ons'

3. Make your offering as wide as possible: try to provide opportunities for ALL to find something that makes them tick.

4. CPD – Try to upskill yourself as often as possible.

5. Enjoy what you do – this is the BEST job in the world.

Y

Younger You!

A common misconception in people considering, or already on, their PE teaching career path is that their role is to mould all pupils into miniature versions of themselves. Truth is, the role is working towards supporting pupils to be the best them, not the best you!

In your role, the appreciation of the breadth of personality, ability, interest, and variance in home support and importance for physical activity and sport must be considered. Don't expect all pupils to mirror the engagement, application, or skill level you have now, or had at their age. I have witnessed trainees becoming frustrated at this, when this can be avoided by an understanding that all your pupils are very different and unique young people.

In these instances, it is important to understand that physical education will have different meanings and connotations for every pupil within a class. From preferences regarding activities being covered, parental influences, and attitudes towards physical activity, to the experiences pupils have had with PE in the past, the range will be vast, and to expect all pupils to have the same natural enthusiasm, passion, and engagement for the same activities, and broader subject, as yourself can be a relatively naïve approach.

My advice here links back to the importance of 'Get to Know Your Pupils'. An in-depth knowledge of a class, and taking time to actively research their previous experiences within physical education in their last school, or during the last academic year, supports activity design. This can also help ensure activities are pitched appropriately to challenge the pupils within the group. Prior to this further research into a class, it will become evident that you are not set to teach 25 clones of yourself. There will be a range of learners, each with their own goal posts, that constitute success in different locations. For some, success is having the confidence to get changed, or join in parts of the warm-up. For others, it will be to successfully perform a backhand serve in badminton, with more failed attempts than good. And, for a few, it will be to apply the serve into a match effectively to outwit an opponent. Do not allow yourself to become frustrated, and classify a lesson as a failure, if all pupils do not reach the most challenging objective of your lesson; appreciate the hundreds of mini successes that, more than likely, occurred due to the diligent, considered, and informed planning that took place prior to the lesson.

Furthermore, it is often important to remember the title of your role. You are employed as a teacher of physical education. As such, you are expected to deliver all elements of the curriculum. You are not employed as a teacher of football, who occasionally dabbles in one or two other activities that you tolerate. Additionally, you might specialise in dance, and have an esteemed dancing background out of school, but you are also expected to get stuck into other curriculum areas. Apologies for the passive aggressive undertones of this rhetoric, but too often I have observed PE teachers safely navigate through an academic year within a bubble of their two or three favourite activity areas. Delivery of this nature is not beneficial to pupils. Pupils in the strongest PE departments access a broad and balanced physical education curriculum, where teaching staff take on the responsibility of ensuring their subject knowledge is comprehensive, and able to address all curriculum areas.

From a personal perspective, and from discussions with colleagues where this is widely acknowledged to be the case, I have found the most rewarding curriculum areas to teach are those away from specialisms. The sense of accomplishment from non-dance specialists that deliver an engaging dance lesson, or a non-rugby specialist that goes away, researches, trains, and then is able to safely deliver tackling contact, is incredible. In PE teaching, confidence breeds confidence. Often, once that first hurdle is cleared, and a lesson is reflected upon as being successful, it stays in the mental filing cabinet for a long time, ready to be accessed when required in the future.

A further consideration that must be addressed accordingly is that many pupils will place differing levels of importance on physical activity, health, exercise, and sport in general by those supporting them at home. Once again, this is likely to differ in most cases to the PE teacher themselves (although granted, not for all) and can lead to bewilderment and even anger when pupils do not reciprocate the same enthusiasm and energy towards their subject. Take a breath, compose yourself, rationalise in your head the contextual levels of success that you are looking to achieve with each pupil, and do your best to work towards these targets through the demonstration of compassionate practice.

In my experience, home attitudes towards physical education come to light in two separate case study examples. There will be the pupils who mirror the poor attitudes towards the subject displayed at home, and there will be the pupils who are enthused by our subject, but lack any form of support from home, and progress can be inhibited as a result.

Firstly, considering the non-supported, non-interested pupils, stay positive, stay calm, and be creative with delivery, lesson design, and style. Break from normal practice and liaise with departmental leads about the possibility of deviating from the curriculum to engage pupils in physical activity. Remember, physical activity is not always 'sport'. As before, success with some pupils is to walk continuously for 5 minutes without stopping – or it might be to participate in a dodgeball, table tennis, yoga, parkour, martial arts, or a fundamental movements programme. Communicating with these pupils, and sharing that you are invested in them, and making them change their attitudes towards physical activity can illustrate that you care, and, sadly, as intimated many times during this book, you might be one of the only people who does.

For the pupil that loves PE, sport, and physical activity, but does not have this attitude shared at home, this is someone that you can have an incredibly powerful impact upon, and make a real difference towards their life. Taking time to celebrate success through praise, rewards, and parental communication can all help to further enhance that love for physical activity. Encouragement of physical activity out of lessons through extra-curricular, or by making that link with local sports clubs could be positive actions you take as a PE teacher to support the development of that pupil. Taking time to reflect on your sporting childhood, your love affair with physical activity, and analysing the similarities and differences to those of pupils in your lessons, is a worthwhile practice. Whilst their personal circumstances will differ to your own, remembering your 'why', and passionately sharing this with pupils through considered teaching, and modelling behaviours that promote healthy and active lifestyles, can be the support mechanisms that pupils need for physical activity to become a positive, lifelong habit.

Whilst the overwhelming rhetoric of this chapter has been to appreciate the differences between pupils and your own attitudes towards physical education, it can be also be worthwhile revisiting your own school experiences to appreciate the strategies and approaches that your PE teachers (often role models that inspire careers in PE teaching) used to motivate and inspire their pupils. Taking yourself back mentally to your own

PE lessons, and reflecting upon the practice of your PE teachers, can be a positive exercise, especially from a more informed position as an adult considering a career teaching PE. Taking time to reflect upon the communication used, methods applied to build relationships, and modelling used from your own PE teachers can be a powerful developmental tool for you personally, as it is supported with an understanding of how these practices made you feel. Similarly, reflecting back to lesser fond PE teachers and other personal learning experiences can provide you with aspects of practice to avoid. Consider how those practices were perceived, and realign them to avoid a repeat of this negative experience for your own pupils.

In conducting this reflection from a personal perspective, I give particular kudos to my outstanding PE teachers from secondary school and college. They ensured that they appreciated the current context of the world, and how it was to be a teenager in the late 90s! They used current trends to engage us, and appreciated that we were developing and growing into young adults; they adapted the way they delivered PE to our developmental stage, and did so seamlessly. This led to seven years of consistent engagement in PE, instead of a tailing off of our enjoyment of the subject, which sadly can often be the case.

Finding a balance between appreciating those elements of your PE experiences that were positive, and provided that 'hook' for the subject, and also appreciating the vast range of pupils that you will be teaching, with their broad differences in attitudes towards physical activity, are both crucial in shaping your planning and approaches throughout your career. As always, proactively reflect, take stock, and move forward.

Top 3 Takeaways!

1. **Prior to delivering out of specialism, request support from a colleague or peer.**
   Ask them to check through your lesson plan for accuracies linked to teaching points pertinent to that activity.

2. **Ensure all planning and preparation is pupil-focused.**
   Consider how all pupils in a lesson will feel during each lesson phase. Ensure activity design is inclusive, and provides appropriate levels of challenge for all pupils within a class.

3. **Explore new and engaging activities, and ideas that can engage different groups of pupils.**
   Consider how to cover traditional curriculum themes with modern and innovative twists.

Chapter Reflection

Kate Thornton-Bousfield, Head of PE and Achievement Youth Sport Trust.
@KLTB26

A fascinating read that both rekindles many memories of my early teaching career, but also highlights our important role as PE teachers in understanding the needs of all learners, and challenging us to use this knowledge to get the best out of them, unlocking their potential through the pedagogical approaches we take to teaching our wonderful subject of PE.

Allow me to reflect on my early days for a moment: teaching in a high performing school, with above average intake, a pretty affluent area, most pupils were involved in after school clubs, house competitions, national competitions, and sports tours aplenty. Sport was a driver for many. A teams, B teams, C teams, Saturday fixtures were the norm and, if I am honest, I think PE became sport. A heavily games-based curriculum, with athletics, tennis, and cricket as the focus in the summer term. But, when I think back, I can see the rolling eyes of some of the girls I taught, when they knew they were going to be doing hockey for the next 6 weeks: they knew there would be a warm up, some skills, a problem for them to solve, a game situation, and some reflection activity. Was I really getting the best out of these learners? Did I consider what they wanted out of the PE lesson? No, probably not; I was focused on the scheme of work, the lesson content in the green folder, and had one eye on who could maybe make the hockey team. I think I did look at the class and think, yes, there are definitely nine or ten mini-me's here.

My view of PE certainly changed when I was timetabled to teach a challenging group of learners. I learned the hard way; my traditional approach was not going to cut it. These learners were not quite as compliant, their needs were very different, and they made sure I knew it! I realised then that PE was not sport, and that the majority of the learners in front of me were never going to want to play sport, but would probably want to be active, healthy, with their friends, and wanted to develop themselves in more than mere physical skills. This is when I became a 'real' PE teacher, when I considered the wider needs of learners, and talked to them about what they wanted from their PE lessons. A learner-centred approach, where the importance of social and cognitive development became more important to me than seeing a pupil perform a complex skill under pressure, which could be done outside of the PE lesson.

I reflected on both the curriculum map and pedagogy. I actually spoke to the learners. Together, we explored how we could get the most out of the time we had, and discussed the purpose of PE. I became a much better teacher for pausing, reflecting, asking, and co-creating. I realised there was not one right way, but many ways to teach PE – it's taking the time to know your learners, and find the right way for them that matters. We learned together, through new activities, for both me and them. We focused on key skills, such as team work, communication, and problem solving. We pushed each other out of our comfort zones. I see many of my past pupils today, each with different memories; for some, we reminisce over the hockey tour to Holland, but with others it's, 'do you remember the time when…'. It's these memories I take a deep breath on – did I give them a positive learning experience, or are they going to remind me of the darker days, when I was not so proud of how I taught? Remember, always…it is how you make a child feel that they will remember.

Z

Z Generation v Alpha Generation

Appreciating the characteristics, lifestyles, interests, and motivations of pupils, from both Generation Z and Generation Alpha, can support lesson planning, delivery style, and overall approaches, maximising engagement of the most unique generations to enter schools in the history of the world!

OK, I will be open and honest – all this categorisation of generations is a new concept to me. That said, the more I read around the characteristics (generally) attributed to each age group, the more my experiences in education resonate, agreeing that the broad descriptors are relatively accurate. Indeed, as a proud 'Millennial' myself, someone that was 'cool' and 'down with the kids' in the late 'noughties', I can concur that I am beginning to be the person I dreaded – that person who struggles to comprehend how adolescents can find their music taste anything other than a 'bloody racket', and fails to interpret the latest fashions, or how to be trendy.

In addition to these quite sad indications that I am getting old (well, late 30's but still), the descriptors linked to my generation are accurate. We are more likely to take risks than other age groups; we do (overall) tend to be ambitious and view competition as a challenge as opposed to a threat; and there is a 'look after number one' vibe, certainly in many of my colleagues, which can sometimes be at a detriment to the 'Teamwork Makes the Dream Work' mantra. Now, once again, not every Millennial has these traits, but becoming aware of how generations can differ due to the world at the time of their childhood and upbringing can help you navigate through the range of interactions you will have with colleagues and pupils on a day-to-day basis.

Chances are, you will be reading as a proud member of the 'Generation Z' (1997 to 2012). Your childhood will have coincided with the development and birth of technologies that continue to be refined today, and will also have an appreciation for the latest trends that pupils, certainly of secondary school age, will be enjoying in their spare time. A lazy assumption and generalisation might be that 'Generation Z' are all 'anti-exercise', with a preference to stay indoors on a games console or smart-phone, as opposed to getting outdoors and exercising. Yes, technology in the household is providing entertainment for this generation to the same end that the Millennials would have to go outside to find, but it is important to avoid generalising across all adolescents, and ensuring that your approaches as a PE teacher encompass the full range of 'Generation Z' pupils.

As mentioned, you will have some pupils that, due to lifestyle habits at home – smart-phone, games console, and tablet culture – likely have a negative relationship with physical activity. And this mentality is likely to be negative also due to these pupils' perception that they will be playing 'catch up' with 'sportier', more active peers. In mixed-lesson settings, differentiation by grouping and activity can be supportive, to help these pupils feel comfortable enough to participate without fear of judgement from peers. A subtle reminder that, once again, success is contextual; you will have 30 individual success targets in each lesson, all different, all impacted by a multitude of factors, including support from home, and previous relationships with physical activity. Be proactive in appreciating and celebrating individual successes, when your knowledge of pupils provides you with the information to do so.

Similar to encouraging a small child to stroke a dog by informing them that the dog will not bite, your role as a practitioner will be to make physical education appealing, and provide pupils with lessons that focus upon slowly building confidence and familiarisation with the sensation of becoming hot and sweaty through exercise. These styles of Generation Z pupils need to feel comfortable in the lesson environment, and will require praise and encouragement. Observing pupils beginning to love their PE lessons from a starting point of worry and disengagement is one of the most rewarding aspects of the role.

In contrast, one positive to highlight from social media culture that Generation Z have grown up with as second nature is accessibility to positive sporting, fitness, and celebrity role models. Often a challenge for this Millennial, but actively ensuring that references are made to the latest positive role models out there can be an excellent motivational tool for pupils. Referring to exercises as performed by a prevalent female celebrity on their social media can engage groups into pushing themselves during health and fitness lessons.

Generation Z have a high awareness of the importance of health and exercise – their online influences commonly refer to training, healthy eating, and exercise habits. Embrace this positivity towards physical activity in your lessons.

Similarly, using sporting role models at the very top of their game, and using them as a discussion point ahead of a lesson, can help focus pupils and provide a challenge to them to emulate their heroes. In my day (once again making myself sound nearer 60 than 37), I often referred to Zinedine Zidane during football lessons, asking pupils to highlight what made him such an outstanding player. Taking time to reference positive people that pupils will see on social media platforms every day can provide an added relevance to content, whilst also portraying (however true this may be) that you are up to speed and relevant yourself!

Teaching content should also aim to be as relevant and in-keeping with trends as possible. Tweaking traditional content to give it a 'Generation Z' twist can result in increased engagement from pupils. Could gymnastics be delivered with a Parkour angle? Dance to incorporate music and routines seen on popular social media apps? Health and fitness lessons that explore the latest exercise trend – CrossFit, or HIIT perhaps? On the fitness topic, Generation Z love technology – could it be incorporated into lessons? Heart rate monitors, pedometers, and self-analysis software could all be woven into lessons to give pupils their technology fix, but also help motivate and focus pupils to burn the most calories or achieve the most steps. A side note to consider, however: I have observed many lessons where a trainee or teaching colleague has been given a target to incorporate ICT into their lesson. Physical activity levels were slashed in favour of tokenistic usage of a tablet or alternative technology. If you are using technology, ensure it is in place to enhance the purpose of the lesson and pupil learning, not simply just to provide an added gimmick to impress observers.

There is, however, another generation even more technologically impacted than the Generation Z: 'Generation Alpha'. The pre-secondary school age pupils that have grown in this world with touch screen technology as the norm – their birth dates pretty much coincide with the invention of the tablet. Devices to watch and find information at their fingertips since they were toddlers. Many of the challenges raised for our Generation Z pupils, especially regarding sedentary tendencies, apply here too, but pupils of this age are the future, and appreciating their developmental journey at primary school can help to inform planning and lesson design at secondary level. Generation Alpha are also the offspring of Millennials. As such, many Millennial ideals are desirable for the Alpha Generation. The challenge here is that, whereas parents might perhaps be keen for exploration, boldness, competition, and challenge, Generation Alpha might not necessarily share this perception of school, and the world in general. Appreciating generational differences between pupils and parents can be vital, especially when communicating with home.

A marked positive when working with Generation Alpha is that, overall, they are conditioned and intrigued to learn. Often referred to as 'screenagers', they commonly spend large amounts of the day being informed, via online streaming or search engines. So, what does this mean for PE? Well, adding themes to lessons such as sports from other countries or cultures, or tying in lessons to current sporting events, can hugely engage Generation Alpha and Z. In addition to the present, using sport and PE to travel back in time can also be a powerful engagement tool. Investigating how PE looked in the same era that a class is learning about in history, or within a novel in English, can also boost engagement. PE can play a hugely impactful role in schools working on a topic-based curriculum, whilst also benefiting from the engagement fostered in other subject areas.

If you are working within secondary, Generation Alpha will be walking through the doors within the next few years. Will your teaching be ready? Do you adapt and review your practice, or keep rolling out the same lessons? If you are teaching the same content in the same way, your teaching will become dated, and not relevant to the current generation (Z or Alpha), and engagement will naturally decline. Teach, Reflect, Adapt, Repeat!

Top 3 Takeaways!

1. **Utilise #eduPE to explore different methods to utilise technology in your lessons.**

2. **Ensure that lessons include information around the benefits of physical activity, and a healthy and active lifestyle.**
   Do not take for granted that pupils will be able to appreciate all the good that PE can do.

3. **Embrace the latest role models and trends.**
   Keep up to date with popular culture, and utilise it to engage your pupils.

Chapter Reflection

Neil McAvoy. Neil has worked with children from zero to eighteen across three continents and six countries over the last three decades. He has been a senior leader in primary schools for nearly two decades, and has always passionately believed in the power of physical activity to transform lives. Having seen Z Generation move through primary schools, Neil has now evolved his curriculum and extra-curricular offer to try and meet the needs of Gen Alpha.
@Neil_McAvoy

So, it would be very easy to dismiss this chapter and all of the research surrounding generations and decide that 'kids are still kids' and 'PE is still PE'. But do you really believe that, or are you reluctant to make changes to your pedagogy, when new generations of pupils and parents are expecting – and, increasingly, demanding – change? During my career, I have seen how different generations of pupils and parents have different needs and demands...and understandably so!

My primary school is now full of Gen Alpha pupils – 'the glass generation' – who are the first individuals where technology was fully ingrained in their lives from birth onwards.

So, what are the implications for physical education teachers and leaders? Clearly, Gen Alpha pupils are used to learning online and, with the increasing growth and use of artificial intelligence, robotics, and augmented reality, as Ben highlights, PE teachers will need to continue to respond and evolve. This includes the contexts we use for learning, especially as 'traditional sports' are becoming less popular and non-traditional sports are rising in popularity, including alternative, adventure,- and e-sports. In addition, recent research that I have carried out revealed how, for a lot of Gen Alpha pupils, PE contexts are expected to help their social and emotional development, with PE being viewed as much more than just physical education.

What is clear is that technology is increasingly key to new learners; therefore, integrating technology will become even more important to engage this generation. Similarly, Gen Alpha learners expect to be communicated with in authentic and transparent ways; plus, with increasingly short attention spans, they require flexibility, and teachers who can innovatively adjust to their needs. In order to be engaged, they expect meaning and purpose behind their learning, and hands-on instead of didactic or teacher-directed experiences in their lessons – something that PE teachers should be able to lead the way in offering.

It is also worth taking a moment to reflect on the parents of Gen Alpha pupils. Research highlights that parents of Gen Alpha children are expecting high quality experiences for their children that they did not necessarily have. They seek choice, seek value, and a differentiated experience. In my school's PESSPA Programme, we acknowledge the insatiable appetite of our pupils and their parents for outstanding experiences, and we are aware that this generation of pupils (and their parents) demand responsive systems of learning to meet the dynamic needs of this tech-savvy generation.

For this generation, it is experience and action that leads to learning – not just instruction and content-based inquiry. Although challenging for schools and teachers, for me, PE departments are among the best-placed to lead on this, and, like Ben highlights, if we don't evolve as practitioners, 'our teaching will become dated and not relevant to the current generation.' The raison d'être for my school's PESSPA Programme is to develop a lifelong love of physical activity: it is our duty to ensure that we continue to evolve and innovate to meet the specific needs of our current and future generations of learners. It is a challenge…but it is an honour!

Final Word

The best job in the world!

PE teaching is the greatest profession possible. The power you have to make such impactful positive change on a young person's life is unrivalled.

This book is designed to provide advice from the shop floor, from a comprehensive secondary school PE department environment that has the most eclectic, talented, resilient, and remarkable young people walk through its changing room doors every day. Our job is to inspire them to fall in love with physical education, or at the very least for them all to appreciate the importance of being healthy and active.

Physical education, educating young people about being physical, is such a crucial, precious, and critical role that we play in the future of individual young people, and will shape the future of the societies in which we live in. This focus upon the future when teaching physical education is vital, and will help shape approach and practice. Hopefully, each chapter has illustrated its importance to the quality of physical education, now and in the future, as we all keep striving to improve, develop, expand, and explore. Take the broader themes of a collection of the chapters within this book. Why is there a real focus upon elements of lesson design? It is because we owe it to the young people that we teach to ensure lessons are underpinned with considered strategy and thought, that the ideas being shared are innovative and exciting, and that the culmination of planned lessons over a term, a year, and through their entire education, is that the young people involved will continue on their journey to love physical activity, exercise, and sport.

Furthermore, the importance of relationships across many contexts has been explored throughout many chapters. Why? Relationships provide the bedrock for solid foundations of practice and delivery to be built upon. Show you care; show you love the special role that you are entrusted to deliver; show that you have that interest in other people to make them better than they were yesterday. Recognise, share, and appreciate contextual success, celebrate, encourage, praise, and make young people feel confident, happy and proud when they run, jump, throw, roll, sweat, stretch, breathe, and move. Ensuring this positivity towards physical activity is, once again, more likely to help us achieve our aim of ensuring active children become active and healthy adults.

PE is a process that begins in early years, and continues all the way through to KS5. Progressive threads along the way all help to stitch together a tapestry that results in a broad, detailed picture of pupils that have a love and passion for our subject. This passion hopefully transcends into pupils leaving school with an appreciation, respect, understanding, and inherent value for physical activity, and the positive impact it makes towards health and well-being. Do not underestimate the importance of our contribution as physical educators. We are making a real difference on so many levels to the pupils in our care.

Overall, I am confident we do a fantastic job. We achieve this by appreciating the complexity of our teaching groups, and the breadth and depth of PE teaching required to engage as many pupils as possible in every lesson. A reminder, however – we are not robotic teaching machines. We will also have ups and downs, good days and bad days, like every human being in every job on the planet. From the outside, and to many, we may appear superhuman, but we all have our vulnerabilities. Acknowledging these is as important as being aware of our strengths. Appreciation of these makes us more effective teachers.

This job isn't just taking a ball outside with a bucket of bibs and saying 'play'. It is not merely facilitation of activity. It is years of dedication, reflection, and sacrifice, but it is absolutely worth it, and there is no better profession. The relationships we build with pupils are crucial. They can be powerful, life-changing, inspiring, and often provide a care and attention for pupils that they do not receive in any other aspect of their lives. Remember this throughout your career: be pupil-focused at all times.

I hope you have enjoyed reading this book as much as I have enjoyed writing it. If one paragraph in one of the chapters helps one person out there, then it will all have been worth it.

Take care and keep learning, keep moving forward and go well comrades...Ben.

Acronym Buster!

PE Teaching is riddled with acronyms! During the early stages of my career, my head was bamboozled with them all. As such, I have attempted to list as many from the world of PE teaching as possible!

Acronym	Full Meaning
AFL	Assessment for Learning
AfPE	Association for Physical education
ASK	Attitude, Skills, Knowledge
BSP	Behaviour Support Plan
BTEC	Business and Technology Education Council
CAMHS	Child and Adolescent Mental Health Service
CCF	Core Content Framework
CNAT	Cambridge National
CPD	Continuing Professional Development
DfE	Department for Education
DPA	Daily Physical Activity
EAL	English as an Additional Language
EBD	Emotional and Behavioural Difficulties
ECM	Every Child Matters
ECF	Early Career Framework
ECT	Early Careers Teacher
EEF	Education Endowment Foundation
ELP	Expected Levels of Progress
EP	Educational Psychologist
EYFS	Early Years Foundation Stage
FE	Further Education
FFT	Fischer Family Trust
GaT	Gifted and Talented
GBA	Games Based Approach
GDPR	General Data Protection Regulation

GTC	General Teaching Council
HBPE	Health Based Physical education
HE	Higher Education
HoDs	Heads of Departments
HRF	Health Related Fitness
IEP	Individual Education Plan
ITT	Initial Teacher Training
KCSIE	Keeping Children Safe in Education
KS	Key Stage
LA	Local Authority
LAC	Looked After Children
LSW	Learning Support Workers
MAT	Multi Academy Trust
MbP	Models Based Practice
MPE	Meaningful Physical education
NQT	Newly Qualified Teacher
NVQ	National Vocational Qualification
OBG	One Big Game
PGCE	Postgraduate Certification of Education
PoS	Programme of Study
PP	Pupil Premium
PPA	Planning, Preparation and Assessment
SEL	Social Emotional Learning
PSHE	Personal, Social and Health Education
QTS	Qualified Teacher Status
SE	Sports Education
SEMH	Social Emotional Mental Health
SENCO	Special Educational Needs Coordinator
SEND	Special Educational Needs and Disabilities
SGO	School Games Organiser
SIMS	School Information Management System
SIP	School Improvement Partner
SLT	Senior Leadership Team
SMSC	Spiritual, Moral, Social and Cultural
SoW	Scheme of Work

SPaG	Spelling, Punctuation and Grammar
SSCo	School Sport Coordinator
SSG	Small Sided Games
SSP	School Sport Partnership
TA	Teaching Assistant
TS	Teaching Standards
TGfU	Teaching Games for Understanding
TLR	Teaching and Learning Responsibility
YST	Youth Sport Trust

Made in the USA
Columbia, SC
03 August 2024

39908159R00100